NUMBERING MY DAYS

Chene Heady

NUMBERING MY DAYS

How the Liturgical Calendar
Rearranged My Life

IGNATIUS PRESS   SAN FRANCISCO

Cover Art and Design by Enrique J. Aguilar Pinto

© 2016 by Ignatius Press, San Francisco
All rights reserved
ISBN 978-1-62164-031-8
Library of Congress Control Number 2015948812
Printed in the United States of America ⊗

CONTENTS

INTRODUCTION:
THE TRIVIAL ROUND,
THE COMMON TASK

I walk into the local coffee shop carrying my year-and-a-half-old daughter, Beatrice, the many pockets of my thin tan trench coat flapping in the fall breeze. "Hi, Bea!" the manager shouts out in her raspy voice when we're barely through the door. She is in her early twenties, with long, untamed wavy brown hair and the affably obnoxious disposition and settled figure of a barfly. She doesn't seem like she would have much interest in families with small children—and, in point of fact, she has never learned my name—but she does have a weakness for Bea ("the only baby I've ever seen who doesn't look like Winston Churchill").

And, as surely as Bea has a weakness for frilly lace dresses, she has a weakness for the coffee shop. She loves the ambient acoustic and jazz music, and, especially, the baked goods. She raises her stuffed flamingo toward the manager as a kind of salute (she never took to a teddy bear). "How's it hanging, Mingo?" the manager barks. Mingo, who is by now a linty blue gray with lingering pink highlights, answers her by jumping up and down. I am apparently the least memorable figure in our entourage.

I order a large coffee, and the manager asks, "What would you like today, Miss Beatrice?"

"A croiss-ant," she replies, in two distinct syllables, each with an emphatic nod of the head that tosses her light brown bob cut back and forth.

I plop Beatrice into the coffee shop's tiny wheeled high chair. She fits easily in the chair, though her long, thin arms and legs stick out in all directions. We careen toward our table, passing it deliberately, then rapidly doubling back, spinning around, and making an abrupt stop exactly at Beatrice's usual seat. She giggles with amusement and whiplash. We annoy only the couple of customers optimistic enough to conduct a job interview in a coffee shop, and we have our fans among the regulars. A rail-thin retired schoolteacher always stops by the table to compliment Beatrice's manners, and a UPS driver with a prominent mustache persistently tries to get conversation out of Mingo.

I pick up our coffee and croissant and return to the table. Out of one of my many pockets, I pull Beatrice's sippy cup of juice; out of another, I grab a copy of the Victorian poet John Keble's collection *The Christian Year*. I begin breaking up the croissant into tiny bits. Beatrice goes right for the croissant, but I have trouble focusing on my book, since I can barely stay awake.

I haven't had a decent night's sleep since my daughter was born. Not long ago, I got my first traffic ticket in sixteen years; head tilted toward the shoulder, eyes just slits, I zoned out and rear-ended a nurse. Now I drink eighty ounces of coffee each day just as a baseline; on truly sleepy days like today, I average about one hundred twenty. My wife, Emily, and I both teach English at colleges in central Virginia (she is also an administrator). I teach mornings and watch Beatrice in the afternoon; Emily teaches afternoons and watches Beatrice in the morning; my wife's parents, who live in town and are retired, graciously cover the interval. I recently realized that my wife and I literally haven't fifteen minutes free a day. Once, on a brief pause between activities, I asked Emily why she was doing the dishes (which is normally my job). "I had ten minutes free and I wasn't going to spend *ten minutes* just sitting around," she replied matter-of-factly. I had to explain to her later why someone else might find this remark funny. We rise at 4:45 A.M. when our daughter starts crying, and we finish our schoolwork and begin our broken sleep at about midnight. Psychologists tell us that dreams often function as a kind of wish fulfillment, compensating for what we feel to be lacking in our daily lives. I have a recurring dream in which I am blissfully asleep.

"Daddy?" Beatrice asks from across the table, snapping me out of my thoughts.

"Yes, Bea?"

"What we doing now, Daddy?"

"How about 'Old McDonald'?" I ask. She nods happily and immediately begins: "Old McDonald adda farm ... yiy, yiy, yiy, yiy, oh!" She loves to talk and she loves to sing; words perpetually bubble out of her. She will gladly sing that song—as nearly as an unusually verbose toddler can enunciate it—over and over again for a good hour. I just have to chime in every once in a while and suggest a new animal ("Rooster? How about rooster?"). If she is particularly agitated, I push her high chair back and forth with my foot.

We're at the coffee shop this afternoon because my wife has a late meeting. I need coffee, I need to reread selections from Keble's *Christian Year* for a class I am teaching on religion and literature, and I need to watch Beatrice. So, of course, I am doing all three things at once. I state the situation to myself plainly: I am shoving bits of croissant at my daughter across the table so she doesn't interrupt me while I work. I am a horrible person.

I open *The Christian Year* to the second poem, "Morning", but I still can't manage to focus. I love my daughter and I love my wife, but mostly I am bored, depressed, and listless. My life is a giant series of tasks to be performed, and most moments are like this one: I focus on no one thing and I am mentally present to no one. I don't want to exaggerate: objectively, nothing has gone dramatically wrong for me, and I have committed no flamboyant sins. Mortal sins generally require planning and commitment, and I have had neither the energy nor the time. But the days drag on, and everything seems empty. I am detached and disaffected, stretched thin and scattered. I feel guilty about feeling this way—I worry that it makes me a bad husband and a bad father—but I can't shake it just by wishing.

"Daddy ...," Beatrice calls out.

"Dog," I reply, and the next verse of "Old McDonald" begins.

Not only do I feel like a bad husband and father, but I feel like a bad Catholic. My sense that the world is meaningless and my life empty simply can't be squared with my Catholic Faith. The Faith declares that *nothing* is without significance. "The world is charged with the grandeur of God", as Gerard Manley Hopkins exclaimed in his poem "God's Grandeur". In the Mass, the priest proclaims that the "fruit of the earth and work of human hands ... will become for us the bread of life", and the "fruit of the vine and work of human hands ... will become our spiritual drink."[1] When we reply, "Blessed be God forever," we affirm that the elements of daily life can, through the power of God, take on a literally divine significance. The trivial and the quantifiable can become the transcendent. But obviously at a gut level, I don't really believe it.

---

[1] "Presentation and Preparation of the Gifts". All quotations in this book from the Order of the Mass or the prayers for the day derive from *The Roman Missal*, English trans. (Washington, D.C.: International Commission on English in the Liturgy, 2010).

Day by day, I transform the transcendent into the trivial and the quantifiable. There is a disconnect between my faith and my life.

"Daddy ...," I hear again from across the table.

"Guinea pig," I answer. Soon there is a "squeak, squeak" both here and there.

I don't have any more time for introspection. I need to take notes on at least a poem or two before Beatrice gets antsy and we need to leave. So I turn to my book and try to read the poem "Morning". The Reverend John Keble was a leader in the Oxford Movement, the Catholic-oriented reform movement in the Church of England; he was one of Blessed John Henry Newman's best friends. His *Christian Year* is structured around the Anglican liturgical calendar and provides a poem for each Sunday, feast day, and special service. Although now largely forgotten, *The Christian Year* was the single best-selling book of poetry of the nineteenth century in England, so it's a logical choice for inclusion in my upper-level course on religion and literature. "Morning", the poem for the Anglican morning service, is the first poem after the "Dedication".

I've read "Morning" before, but today it speaks to my life. The speaker describes an objectively ideal morning—a beautiful sunrise, with a gentle breeze, slight fog, and lots of dew—but admits that personally he feels no connection to this scene and derives no sense of meaning from it. His is a "dark, void spirit", as he has already lamented in the "Dedication". He believes in Christianity but feels like he lives in a meaningless world. All he has going for him is that he knows that he has a problem, and he suspects that problem is with him and not God or the world. The speaker directly addresses the sunrise, breeze, and fog to ask them why they bother to show themselves to

disaffected, listless humanity at all: "Why waste your treasures of delight / Upon our thankless, joyless sight ...?"
(lines 13–14).

"Daddy ..."

"Yak," I reply at random. Soon Beatrice is calling out,
"With a yak, yak here and a yak, yak there, here a yak,
there a yak ..."

Keble starts where I start. But he ends somewhere very
different from where I end. This poem concludes with
the speaker imploring God to "help us, this and every
day, / To live more nearly as we pray" (lines 63–64). The
solution for a meaningless life, Keble asserts, is to internalize the liturgy, the daily prayer of the Church. Keble
believed that when the undivided early Church devised
the liturgical year she was expressing a legitimate insight
into the mind of God. The liturgical year offers a method
of experiencing time and creation in which all things are
invested with meaning; divine time (*kairos*) replaces empty
time (*chronos*). Through the liturgical year and its daily
prayers and scriptural readings, the Church teaches us how
to read the temporal in light of the eternal.

But most Christians, Keble thought, fail to take advantage of the Church calendar. Most of us live lives that seem
devoid of meaning precisely because we have abandoned
liturgical time. The calendar we actually live is one structured around the work week, not around the Resurrection
of Christ (Sunday, the Christian Sabbath) or God's rest at
the end of the creation of the world (Saturday, the Jewish
Sabbath). In the clock we've internalized, all moments are
equally insignificant, divided only between work (Monday–
Friday) and leisure (Saturday–Sunday). It's no coincidence
that we see ourselves as producers and consumers rather
than as divine creations. Keble wrote his book of poems as
an attempt to break people out of this pattern; he wanted to

show his readers how an individual's life and world would change if he really tried to live the liturgical year.

"Daddy, please ..."

"Lion," I shoot back without thinking. Beatrice likes lions and does not ask what they are doing on a farm; she merely roars. I push the high chair back and forth with my foot. I'm running out of time, and I seem to be near a breakthrough.

The speaker of "Morning" begins to break out of his disaffection and depression precisely because he has initiated his experiment in liturgical living. His goal, that "on our daily course our mind / Be set to hallow all we find" (lines 29–30), should be ours as well. The liturgical calendar teaches us to see our lives in light of Scripture and of the stories of Christ and the saints; through the liturgical calendar each moment stands revealed as a thing sacred, containing its own revelation from God. If we were to seek this sacral sense of time and place, then even "Life's dullest, dreariest walk" would become merely another occasion through which God could reveal wisdom to our hearts (lines 47–48). If we could only live as we pray in the liturgy, then nothing would be banal, pointless, and dull; or, better, all things banal, pointless, and dull would themselves become paths to the divine:

> The trivial round, the common task,
> Would furnish all we ought to ask
> Room to deny ourselves; a road
> To bring us daily nearer God. (lines 53–56)

"Daddy?"

"A road," I suggest, my mind still on the poem.

"No noise," she objects, her brow furrowed, her eyes intense.

"Breeze, then," I counter, still thinking of Keble.

"How does a breeze go?"

"Whoosh." Beatrice breaks into a slight smirk. She likes that sound. Soon there is a "whoosh, whoosh" everywhere, and in fact the Spirit may be moving. What if instead of studying Keble as an academic subject, I actually tried to live out his ideas? Could my life be altered if I tried to live the liturgical year in the way that Keble—and Pope [Emeritus] Benedict XVI and Dietrich von Hildebrand and others—would suggest?

So, sitting in the coffee shop, feeding my daughter croissant, and listening to Frank Sinatra's cool jazz mingle with the persistent refrain of "Old McDonald", I decide to take Keble's book as a challenge. The new liturgical year is about to begin, and I will spend the next year trying to see my life in light of the liturgy. Each day of the year to come (2011–2012, Cycle B), I will write a meditation relating the day's liturgical readings and prayers to my thoughts and to my life. And, at the end of the year, I will see if there is any change in how I see myself and the world, and determine whether my life has been altered.

I stick the book and sippy cup back into two of the many pockets of my coat, I feed Beatrice her last bit of croissant, I race her back across the restaurant in her high chair, and I pull her out and prop her up against my shoulder. I walk out into the parking lot, not yet in any way a new man, but eager to see what might happen if I lived more nearly as I prayed.

Through all the difficulties of the next year, I stayed true to my quest, and this book is the result. The ruminations that follow were written in real time, on the days of the liturgical year recorded below; I wrote an entry for every day of the Church year. The prose was cleaned up later for the sake of readability, but the thoughts of the day belong to the day. Also for the sake of readability, I have omitted entries that repeat ideas and themes found elsewhere in the book or that now strike me as irrelevant to the main narrative.

One note: As you read my ruminations and my stories, you may not always find my thoughts and actions to be morally heroic. Some of you may already be holier Catholics as you begin reading this book than I will manage to become by the end of it. Some of you may be shocked that it took me a whole liturgical year to come to realizations that for you would have been obvious and decisions that for you would have been automatic.

But that's okay. For I am not the hero of this book— the liturgical year is, and I am its often-bumbling sidekick. If my experience and reflections are of any value, it will be due more often to my faults than to my virtues. In *The Joy of the Gospel*, Pope Francis teaches that the liturgy is a means by which "the Church evangelizes and is herself evangelized."[2] You will be watching the liturgy evangelize me. If I feel stretched thin and like my life is devoid of meaning, then studies suggest I'm just the average adult American. If my faith does not shape my life in the way it should, then polls suggest I am an average Catholic. If the liturgy alters my imperfect existence, it can alter yours. The liturgy is our universal story.

---

[2] Francis, apostolic exhortation *Evangelii Gaudium* [The joy of the gospel] (Vatican City: Libreria Editrice Vaticana, 2013), paragraph 24, Holy See website, http://w2.vatican.va/content/francesco/en/apost_exhortations/documents/papa-francesco_esortazione-ap_20131124_evangelii-gaudium.html.

THE HOLY FAMILY AND,
WELL, MY FAMILY
(Advent and Christmas Time)

Tuesday of the First Week in Advent (Lk 10:21–24)

I begin this liturgical year knowing that I don't yet get liturgical time. I go to Mass every week. I am more or less aware of the Church calendar, more or less by accident. My parish is like any other: every December there is a folding table in the narthex piled high with free calendars that erase the fine line between religious art and advertisements for funeral homes. I've never been one to pass up anything that's free, and I've never been one to fail to use whatever I've got; so I can find out what saint's day it is just by looking up at the wall calendar.

But I know that I have not internalized liturgical time; it's not part of who I am. I have, however, internalized clock time. Even on those rare occasions when my daughter sleeps in, I inevitably wake at 4:45 A.M., fifteen minutes before the alarm. The alarm clock has become part of me; I don't even need to hear it. And once I'm up, I live by the law of the Microsoft Outlook Calendar. It divides my life into a series of tasks and shouts at me with persistent reminders as they approach and pass (the computer rings like a doorbell, and a pop-up informs me: "Reminder:

Appointment: Pick up your daughter: 15 minutes ago"). Once a task is done, it's "dismissed". And then the next task pops up.

The Outlook Calendar is a more palatable, white-collar version of the manifold beepers and buzzers of a fast-food restaurant—as I know all too well. I paid my own way through the cheapest Catholic college in Michigan by living with my mother and working untold hours at a series of fast-food restaurants in suburban Detroit. Every time a run of meat was done cooking, a beeper screamed across the kitchen. A higher-pitched wail meant a basket of fries. A low buzzer meant a round of buns. A persistent bleating like Morse code meant a customer waiting on drive-through. And all too often, all beepers and buzzers went off simultaneously, in a mad cacophony. Then, thought was impossible, and life had only one goal: to shut the stupid things off. Not everyone could psychologically handle this. At one such moment, a cook—a wan high school student with dyed black hair—collapsed into a weeping, huddled mass on the floor; he was led out the door and never came back. I'm not so sensitive, but even I used to feel like Pavlov's dog. When the phone at home beeped at me, I answered without thinking, "Welcome to the drive-through. May I take your order?"

The Outlook Calendar, though less obnoxious and somewhat subtler than a fast-food beeper, is functionally no different. It really does imply a basically Pavlovian view of humanity: we are just animals responding to stimuli, completely finite creatures devoid of agency and will. Only the tangible and the immediate, only what shouts and beeps at us, is real; nothing transcendent exists, and there is no purpose in recollection.

The liturgical calendar asks me to back up from the moment, to see larger patterns, to read the moments of my day in light especially of the graced moment of the Incarnation, to consider the possibility that, metaphorically, all moments are incarnational. Christ is the key to understanding existence, and the liturgical year asks me to juxtapose Christ's life and teachings with the day-to-day life I live. If I really do that, God will, in the words of today's Alleluia, "enlighten the eyes of his servant[ ]". As today's Gospel (Lk 10:21–24) proclaims, since "all things have been handed over" by God to Christ his Son, if we know and meditate on Christ, we will come to understand things "hidden" from "the wise and the learned" (21–22).[1]

But the liturgical calendar has this great disadvantage over the Outlook Calendar: it can't shout at me. So I've tried to help the liturgical year along by signing up for a free e-mail service that sends me the daily Mass readings. If contemplation—breaking the habit of seeing life as a series of tasks—becomes itself a task that I must tackle as I clean out my e-mail in-box, perhaps I can begin to learn to enter into divine time.

Friday of the First Week in Advent (Is 29:17–24)

Isaiah offers a magnificent vision of divine restoration: the day will come when the blind shall see, the poor will be exalted, and the desert will be fruitful (Is 29:17–24, today's first reading). But one of his many images of restoration

---

[1] Since this book is a meditation on the liturgical year, all scriptural quotations, unless otherwise noted, are taken from *Lectionary for Mass for Use in the Dioceses of the United States of America*, 2nd typical ed. (Washington, D.C.: Confraternity for Christian Doctrine, 2001). In the heading for each daily entry, I will identify in parentheses the particular text or texts from the lectionary that will serve as a subject for rumination.

strikes me strangely: "On that day the deaf shall hear / the words of a book" (18).

You see the problem: yes, it would be a divine miracle if the deaf heard "the words of a book". Deaf people can't hear. But God's miracles have meaning; they are signs, they signify. And what's the purpose here? What's the point? Deaf people can read already. If anything, silent reading is faster and leads to better retention. So what's the good of them hearing the words of a book? For that matter, when does *anyone* need to hear the words of a book?

Unfortunately, I might know the answer. We hear the words of a book when the Gospel is read at Mass. Except I usually don't—not anymore. My daughter, Beatrice, is a very active one-and-a-half-year-old. And my wife, Emily, and I spend all of Mass just trying to get her through it. Last Sunday, Beatrice bolted twice from the pew, once to try to hug the statue of the Virgin Mary, once to dash up the aisle for a loud conversation with the Crucified Christ. "Mo" is her word for "more", and she loves the sound of the word "amen". Throughout Mass, each solemn moment of silence following a liturgical prayer is punctuated with the shout, "Mo! Mo amen!" All of this is charming, and I hope it shows a developing love for the Faith. But if it's your job to keep Beatrice interested and quiet so that other people can follow the service, there is really little chance of your hearing much of it yourself. I have to hope that it counts for something spiritually that I'm there at all. And, during the closing hymn—if she has managed to make it that far—Bea erupts with a scream and a cry, and we have to beat a hasty retreat. Emily, ever the planner, benevolent administrator of both her academic division and the lives of all those around her, has already snatched up our scattered gear and crammed it into a backpack; I'm swinging the car seat like a pendulum in a mad dash for the exit.

It's important that we hear the words of a book. The book of Isaiah was written in an oral culture; a book was to be read aloud. As late as Saint Augustine's time, people typically read aloud even when they were alone (Augustine was freaked out the first time he met someone who read silently). The purpose of a book was to capture a living human voice and insight and convey it to a community; similarly, the purpose of a prophecy like Isaiah's was to capture the actual voice of God and to summon a community around it. When King Josiah recovered the Law (see 2 Kings 22), it was read aloud to the whole city, and the whole community responded. Everyone, without exception, needs to gather together, and everyone, without exception, needs to hear. Mass may be the last place where oral reading still has this ancient meaning and significance.

We need to hear the words of a book; we need to be summoned together as a community, as the People of God. But I don't know if I really do hear or if the Church has really become my community. I'm distracted during Mass, and the mad dash out the door with our screaming child means that I never stay for communal coffee and doughnuts afterward, to get to know people, to talk. In point of fact, I spend two hours a day driving to and from work, which has made it easy to have little loyalty to the place where I work and the place where I reside. Like most Americans, I love my family and work hard at my job, but beyond that I'm an individualist with weak communal ties. I'm always thinking about joining a parish group or a parish ministry but always decide I'm too busy and put it off to another time. The prophet imagines a restored community where all *hear* the Scriptures together and are transformed by them. The Church's liturgical year resonates with Isaiah's vision. But as yet, I don't.

Monday of the Second Week in Advent
(Is 35:1–10; Lk 5:17–26)

Today in the Gospel, Jesus heals a paralytic and forgives his sins, fulfilling the prophecy found in Isaiah that the day would come when "the lame" would "leap like a stag" (Is 35:6). In return, the Pharisees accuse Jesus of blasphemy.

I often think about the Pharisees and ruminate on their rejection of Jesus. I find it difficult to dismiss them out of hand, perhaps because I am myself a scholar by trade; I teach at a small public teachers college. The Pharisees were the great scholars of their time and place. Shortly after the composition of the New Testament, the next generations of Pharisees wrote the Talmud, both one of the masterpieces of world religion and a virtuoso work of literary interpretation. Who knew the prophecies of Isaiah better than they did? Who was more capable of interpreting them? Who dreamed more intensely of their fulfillment? They had knowledge, devotion, zeal. How could they have missed the mark?

I wonder whether the sad truth—about both the Pharisees and us—is that we don't really want our hopes fulfilled. When God actually fulfills his word, our world changes. If miracles do happen, there is nothing in this world that can be taken for granted. When Jesus heals physical deformity, he is showing that we're encountering the one originally responsible for the type, the form, the shape of humanity, that we're getting in touch with ultimate things. This is exhilarating—but it's also terrifying. The Israelites begged Moses to *stop* God from speaking directly to them (see

Ex 20:18–19). If God can take the form of a person, he is getting dangerously close to me and can ask questions I would rather not answer and make demands I would rather avoid.

For the last six years, I have tried to live my Catholic Faith very openly as a professor at a public college where (as at other public colleges) faith itself is often under assault. But I can't teach every student, and although my faith informs my teaching, there are legal limitations to what I can explicitly say in front of the classroom. I have been a guest speaker for campus ministries, both Catholic and Protestant. I know how important campus ministries are, especially at secular universities; I converted to Catholicism during college and did my graduate work at a major public institution. But I long prayed for an opportunity to share my faith on a wider scale, in some form the whole campus could not possibly miss, although I couldn't imagine what form that would take.

This March, I received an e-mail informing me that my college was going to require all incoming freshmen to read an anthology of essays called *This I Believe*, in which famous people discuss their personal beliefs—which are almost uniformly irreligious. All freshmen would then be required to write "belief statements" in their Introduction to College class. To introduce the students to the campus and to provide them with model essays, the university would open the fall semester with an evening pep rally of sorts in which a group of select faculty would read their own belief statements to all incoming freshmen. Volunteers were needed.

I didn't even consider it. I had a small child and wanted to be home in the evenings. I had colleagues who put up with my private professions of faith but would consider a public profession to be an act of aggression, even a violation of the separation of church and state. I didn't care greatly about their opinions but knew that if they got too angry, they could make it difficult for me to do my job—and profess my faith at the university—in the future. In short, if I volunteered, my life would get more complicated, and I didn't have the time. The opportunity I had long been praying for had presented itself, and I just deleted the e-mail and went back to grading a stack of papers.

A few days later, a fellow Catholic forwarded the e-mail to me, assuming I hadn't gotten it. He wrote, "Someone needs to do this. We can't have a 'belief night' without anyone professing the Faith. I'm new at the college. Too risky for me. It's got to be you." Still seeking an escape, I drove home to our cozy little English cottage and asked my wife. "There's no way I can do this, right?" I said. "You need my help taking care of our daughter." Unfortunately, Emily has a very strong sense of duty. It's one of her defining traits. It's one of the first things I noticed about her: petite, brunette, quick-witted, duty bound. (Once we began dating, I quickly nicknamed her Pia Emilia [Emily bound by duty], and the nickname still fits.) She said, "You need to go. It's a divine appointment. I've got things covered at home."

So, after listening to other faculty talk about how they believed in women's rights, or free speech, or not being a jerk, I stood in front of a massive auditorium full of eighteen-year-olds, wearing one of my two sport coats, and proclaimed, "I'm a Catholic." I then went on to explain why I believe in the universal Church and why the world needs the Church. I had fulfilled a dream I had long had of giving witness to my faith—entirely against my will. We think we want life and wholeness. But when Jesus tries to give them to us, we often try to talk our way out of it.

Thursday of the Third Week in Advent (Is 54:1–10)

I am beginning to understand that in trying to learn to think with the liturgy, I am also trying to learn the shape of the world. If in the Incarnation God really became man, then Advent marks the reestablishment, the refounding, of the world. A fallen, chaotic, and often seemingly purposeless world will no longer be left to function on its own terms. Jesus, as Paul teaches, is the new Adam, and the Holy Spirit is again hovering over the face of the waters. The world is being remade, and given new form, its proper and true form, as willed by the Creator.

Today Isaiah foretells the spiritual restoration for which at our deepest levels we long, though we sometimes foolishly resist it. A great poet, he depicts the scene visually and orally: the barren woman, past all hope, discovers she has suddenly become abundantly, prolifically fertile and can't keep from singing out her joy (Is 54:1). But how disconnected and severed we've become from this particular metaphor! We live in a culture that actually worships barrenness; childlessness is promoted as an ecologically responsible, financially wise, and generally ethically superior lifestyle choice. To us, fertility isn't a restoration, and barrenness isn't a tragedy. Contrast Isaiah with the conclusion of one of the most quoted poems of the second half of the twentieth century ("This Be the Verse" by the English poet Philip Larkin):

> Man hands on misery to man
> > It deepens like a coastal shelf
> Get out as early as you can
> > And don't have any kids yourself.

I understand the modern embrace of barrenness—you can control and plan a sterile world better. The fewer people, the fewer variables. Even on an individual level, a married couple without kids can more easily plan and apportion resources and set a course for life—whereas one never really knows what a kid will do or require next. "Planned Parenthood" is a euphemism for abortion, and perhaps rightly so, since if there is one thing that can't be planned, it's parenthood; the only way to set the course of a child's existence definitively is to prevent him from coming into the world at all.

I am a child of my culture and am as skittish about fertility as anyone. Like most members of the so-called Generation X, I am the product of divorce. My father left my mother for a mistress (a coworker from the same automotive factory, a true Detroit story) when I was a teenager, and our family was not exactly a set of Precious Moments figurines before that. I'm all too acutely aware of everything that can go wrong with home and family. So I was nearing thirty by the time I entered the state of marriage. (My wife confesses that she had begun to despair of ever getting a proposal from me. When I finished proposing, she embraced me tightly, stretched her head up to my shoulder, and whispered in my ear, "Well, it's about time.") Even then, Emily and I delayed having children for nine years, in part so we could complete graduate school and get our careers established, in part because we were simply afraid. This is a typical story, and my wife and I are different from the secular world around us only in that we used Natural Family Planning to achieve these ends.

Put it all together, and I was almost thirty-eight by the time I became a father. Even then, I wasn't brimming over with parental emotion. I participated in the conception and rearing of offspring only as a matter of dogma—a remarkably unsentimental and possibly unnatural statement, I know, but no exaggeration. In *Heretics*,

G. K. Chesterton observed that in the modern age, an age when "everything will be denied", everything—even things that should be by nature visible and obvious—must "become a creed". The generative nature of marriage can serve as a good example.

Here's how I came to have a child: I believe in the infallibility of the Church as both sound deduction and sound doctrine. I believe in my own fallibility as a clear conclusion from empirical evidence. If my instincts and emotions conflict with Church teaching, I know that the smart money is on the Church. So I trusted that the Church, which says that Christian love is by definition fertile and productive and requires openness to children as a condition for a valid marriage, understood more about love than I did. We listened to the Church and had a child. Everything will become a creed. (Still, there are limits to our virtue and fecundity. We currently have no plans for a second child.)

By the time my wife and I had our daughter, everyone we knew had already assumed that we had deliberately opted against children. When I announced that Emily was pregnant, my public college professor colleagues did not, like the woman in Isaiah, break into song. In fact, upon hearing the news, one professor jumped up from my spare office chair, quietly closed the door, leaned forward until our faces were almost touching, and dramatically whispered, "Was it planned? Are you happy about it?"

I write in Ohio from a hotel with a splendid view of the airport parking lot. I am traveling to see my family in Michigan for Christmas; this is the first holiday season of which our daughter will be consciously aware. Beatrice is a force of nature who obviously had to exist; if I needed the Church to tell me to procreate, this fact reflects as favorably on the Church's wisdom as it does poorly on my own. Beatrice constantly upsets my plans—but in a way that challenges the more mistaken parts of my values and that makes a new world. She is a new voice that must be taken into account and cannot simply be controlled, predicted, or otherwise stifled. She will speak to anyone, at the most inappropriate times, offering loud pleasantries to the middle-aged man busy crying after church in front of the columbarium that contains his mothers ashes. She will do anything for a laugh, and shouts, "Humbug!" every time someone wishes her, "Merry Christmas!" She has no idea what the word means, but it always works. The blessings of parenthood are many, though they cannot be graphed on a chart.

And this is exactly how the metaphor in Isaiah works. The coming of the Kingdom of God is the coming of a new world, one that transforms us and changes our expectations. This is precisely why many resisted it then—Herod, for one, preferred that parenthood be precisely planned, so as to fit perfectly into the existing political and economic structures—and why many (and even some unredeemed part of myself) still resist it now.

December 22 (Weekdays of Advent from December 17 to 24) (1 Sam 1:24–28; 1 Sam 2:1, 4–5, 6–7, 8abcd)

The first chapter of Samuel tells the story of Hannah, a woman who has grieved throughout her married life over her inability to bear a child (1 Sam 1:5–7). In desperation, she goes to the house of the Lord at Shiloh to implore God for a son and prays with such raw and unfiltered emotion that the priest mistakenly thinks she is drunk (14). She promises God that if he gives her a son, she will return the gift to him, dedicating the child to God's service all his days. God grants her prayer; she bears a son, Samuel (19–20).

In today's first reading (1 Sam 1:24–28), Hannah fulfills her vow. She leaves the young Samuel at the temple, giving him over forever to its service; the priest Eli will raise him from now on. I can follow the logic behind Hannah's action. Our children are not just physical bodies, reflections of their parents' DNA; they are utterly individual immortal souls. As immortal souls, they are not merely products of their parents' will or desire; they are gifts from God (11). Since we did not simply make our children, we do not have absolute rights over them. We cannot keep them forever as our own.

I get the logic. I'm willing to grant that God created my child, not I. Especially since Beatrice learned to talk, it has been easy for me to imagine that my role in producing her was incidental. She continually comes out with statements I never would have made, displaying even at the age of one and a half an absurdist humor all her own. Lying on her black wooden changing table and staring at an extreme close-up of a cow's face framed on the wall above, she explains that a *cow*, not a bunny, "goes hop, hop, hop". Then she giggles uncontrollably. With variations such as "Bunny goes tweet" and "Birdie goes moo", this can continue for hours. She is clearly other than me, and I can't claim to follow her thoughts. She is an immortal soul. She is not simply the product of my DNA. I am the occasion of her existence, not the cause.

As I said, I get the logic—but I can't fathom how Hannah did it, how she summoned up the courage to perform this act of surrender. I did not implore God for a child as she did, but now that I have a daughter of my own, I cannot imagine giving her up, forsaking all parental rights and duties. I understand now, as I never have before, why

parents set extensive rules for their children and micro-
manage their academics and extracurricular activities. It's
terrifying to realize that in the end you can do little to
determine your child's destiny in life; despite your best
efforts, you can help only so much. Any prop that produces an illusory sense of control and allows you to fend
off this fear is welcome.

I understand this terror in my very bones. As absurd as
it sounds, I literally was driven to tears the first time my
daughter was bitten by a mosquito. We had her strapped
in her tan stroller waiting for a walk on a hot Southern
summer day. I stepped away for a second to hook the dog
on her leash, then turned back and saw a mosquito making
a feast of my daughter's cheek. Beatrice didn't even think
to cry. She tried to move her hands, but they fluttered
at her sides, nowhere near the placid, content, blissfully
undisturbed bug. As I chased the mosquito away, I found
myself crying.

I am not a crier. I have buried relatives without shed-
ding a tear. But that day I wept. Beatrice's level of vulnerability was unthinkable: she couldn't even shoo away
a bug that was eating her face. How could anyone be that
helpless? How could she ever be let loose in the world?
And if I can't protect her from such a small-scale piece of
adversity as a hungry mosquito, what use will I be when it
comes to larger matters?

Hannah is made of sterner stuff than I. She can give
Samuel up because she understands, as she prays in today's
Responsorial Psalm (1 Sam 2:1, 4–5, 6–7, 8abcd), that "the
Lord puts to death and gives life" (6); the aspects of life
that we can control are strictly limited. If I refuse to admit
this, I will end up harming both myself and my daughter.
A Samuel who stays home with his doting parents does
not judge Israel, does not anoint King David, does not

point the way to the Messiah. Nor does a Jesus whom an overprotective Mary shields from the Cross. We all must surrender our children to God; Hannah's action is one we all at some point must perform. Only thus does the Kingdom come.

December 24 (Weekdays of Advent from December 17 to 24) (Lk 1:67–79)

The entrance antiphon for today is "Behold, when the fullness of time had come, / God sent his Son into the world." The phrase "fullness of time" refers to the Greek concept of *kairos*, or rhetorical timing. The art of persuasion depends not just on saying the right thing—or even the right thing to the right person—but on saying the right thing to the right person at the right time. Rhetoric or persuasion often gets a bad name, but it is not just the purview of used-car salesmen and politicians. The book of Proverbs associates rhetorical skill, especially rhetorical timing, with wisdom and is always offering advice about what to say—or what not to say—and when to say it. What each person can actually hear depends on where he is in life. A word in season to my bohemian cousin, an artist who lives in a loft in downtown Detroit, would be different from a word in season to my Evangelical Protestant aunt, a pastor's wife who lives in Indiana. It's a basic spiritual truth.

God himself, the author of all wisdom, considers timing and his audience when he speaks to the world; he speaks to be heard. Blessed John Henry Newman considered this to be a central aspect of God's compassionate dealings with humanity. God teaches his lessons to us gradually and in ways we can understand. Newman called this the "economy". And God's *kairos*, his rhetorical timing, is

perfect. As the Gospel reading for today reminds us, thousands of years prior to the Incarnation, back in the days of
Abraham, God was already preparing the way for Jesus'
coming (Lk 1:73). But he waits for the fullness of time
to act.

I can admire God's timing all the more because my
wife and I both lack *kairos*. Emily is an energetic, effective,
hyperorganized academic administrator. She has a compassionate heart and is a fixer. She can't leave any problem unresolved; if she cares about you, she'll start breaking
your troubles down into quantifiable terms and will soon
produce a detailed plan—often with an accompanying
spreadsheet—to show you how to fix them. Her answer as
to when something should be done is always "Now." We
have a vintage gateleg dining-room table that we picked
up for cheap at an antique store. Emily remarked to me
one day at breakfast, "That leg looks a little wobbly." I
agreed, and went on with my breakfast. We had a full
day of work ahead of us, and the table wasn't collapsing
yet. Around five o'clock, I walked in the door with my
briefcase and found her lying under the table with a drill in
her hand and wood screws in her teeth. Her approach to
people is similar. She once tried to help an impoverished,
only partly literate woman who desperately needed public assistance. The woman fell into a flat-out panic when
Emily plopped a giant pile of government forms in front
of her and cheerfully said, "Let's get to work." And, if
right now I'm a bit withdrawn and we're both a bit short
with each other, Emily is again ready with an immediate,
tangible answer: "People get like that when they have no
personal space. We need a bigger house. I could call a few
real estate agents I know."

I am more hesitant and skeptical about my own plans and
intentions. As I will narrate later, the main achievements of

my life haven't been the results of good planning or careful design, and the aims I have carefully pursued have often been thwarted—mercifully so. I always doubt whether I truly understand a situation or know what should be done. So my response is always "Wait." The laundry sink in the basement drips slightly around the drain seal. My solution: wait and see if miniscule sediment from the washing machine gradually plugs the leak. If we try to fix it now, it might just make things worse. And I take the same approach to people. I grew up in working-class Michigan, surrounded by people who had seemingly intractable problems—frequently economic, often chemical, sometimes psychological—and who were frankly and unapologetically open about them. But as proud, independent Midwesterners, they also considered all attempts to rescue them from their problems to be intrusive, condescending, and basically insulting. Until they had reached the end of their rope, they would meet your good intentions with curses. So I'm always urging Emily to wait and delay action until things get worse. And, of course, this is also my response to her desire to call a real estate agent: "Let's not rush into anything. The problem might not be the house. It might be us, in which case a new house won't fix anything. Let's wait and see" (I know this discussion is far from over; the conflict is only delayed).

Emily's answer is always "Now", and mine is always "Wait." Neither is God's response. In my wife's timing, Jesus would come into the world ten minutes after the fall of humanity, before the angel with the flaming sword has even been properly positioned in front of the gates of Eden. Surely, the world couldn't just be left to suffer. But we had to experience sin, humanity's enormous capacity for self-alienation and self-destruction, to understand our need for a Savior. And we had to come to understand the nature of God in broad strokes through the Jewish covenant before we could recognize his subtler portrait in Jesus. We hear as according to our capacity we can.

On the other hand, in my timing, Jesus wouldn't have come even now. I would never deem humanity ready to receive his message. I would wait for a total collapse of civilization, some seemingly unmistakable sign that would illustrate that none of our attempts at Babel could ever succeed, that we could not be as gods (nuclear annihilation might best fit the bill). I would always want another four or five prophets to come and explain God's intentions even more clearly, to ensure that the point could not be missed even by the most resistant of audiences. And redemption would never come.

Christ comes when the prophets have prepared the way so that the Jewish people, if they are willing, are capable of understanding his person and message. He comes when Greek and Roman thinkers like Plato and Cicero have turned the thoughts of the pagan world toward the Absolute, toward ethics, toward even the idea that the man who speaks the truth must suffer and die. He comes late enough that he might be understood, and early enough that humanity still has time to act.

Today, I took my daughter to the Christmas pageant performed each year by the children of the parish. My wife and I have read Beatrice board-book versions of the Christmas story, but she does not yet have either the attention span or the vocabulary to follow the pageant's plot. Still, she loved the shepherds' flowing outfits, and she loved the drums the shepherds inexplicably beat as they processed into the church and up the aisle (a dubious method of shepherding if ever there was one). She happily beat on the pew in time. God speaks to her, as he speaks to us, in the terms that resonate with her. Even now she begins to move in the rhythms of faith, which she will better understand later. Christ has come. God's redemption has begun. And we won't fully grasp its import until he comes again.

Feast of Saint John the Apostle (December 27)
(1 Jn 1:1–4)

In the last ten days, I've had to consume seven absolutely enormous multicourse meals, followed up by more candy and cookies than I'm likely to eat for the next ten months. As divorce and geography divide and disperse the American family, meals strangely multiply. What would once have been two family gatherings—one for my side of the family and one for my wife's—now more than triples. We must separately visit in Michigan the residences of my mother, my father and stepmother, my maternal aunt, and my paternal grandfather; in Ohio, the residences of my wife's maternal aunt and uncle and paternal aunt and uncle; and in Virginia, the residence of my wife's parents.

As each door opens, piles of food materialize, ranging from the heights of homemade roast turkey, ham, and Yankee pot roast down to the depths of build-your-own deli sandwiches and even a bag of fast-food tacos. Seconds are more or less mandatory and chased with innumerable plates of cookies and perhaps cream puffs. Then everyone grabs a cup of coffee and, crammed in at close quarters, awkwardly discusses the year. I get to hear about my cousins' jobs handling toxic waste and tending bar; in return, my cousins have to pretend not to be bored by my stories about teaching.

As I discreetly crack open a window and try to fend off nausea, I find myself wondering—as so many people do this time of year—what does any of this have to do with Christ? What could eating yourself sick and making awkward small talk possibly have to do with Jesus, the meek and lowly Savior, the Divine Word?

The Church answers with today's Feast of Saint John, the mystic of tangibility. As related in the book of Revelation, John saw majestic visions of eternity whose contents the rest of us can't really even begin to comprehend. But John understood the Incarnation too well to have his head in the clouds; his emphasis is always on corporeality. He tells us in today's epistle (1 Jn 1:1–4) that in the Incarnation God literally handed himself over to humanity. The "Word of life ... was made visible" and was "looked upon and touched with our hands" (1–2). An inconceivable thought. The eternal God made himself a being who could be handled, a baby who could be passed around at parties. He entered into our mess to be handled, because only by turning himself over to us could he really have "fellowship with us" and create a divine community through which his followers, and eventually the world, might be redeemed (3). And from the moment Christ entered on this mission of descent and vulnerability, he has never looked back. He is still passed around and handled (not always delicately) at Mass and still binds all those who dare touch him into a fellowship, a holy community.

My own familial gatherings—as mixed as they are, with a troubled cousin or a scapegrace uncle for every saintly aunt—partake to a lesser degree of this community if there is even an ounce of faith in us (and there is at least an ounce there). When I long to escape these gatherings and to evade the endless plates of food—which are, after all, the physical signs of our shared fellowship—I am quite literally holding myself more distant and aloof than

God himself. The jostle of contact that comes with the holidays in these overcrowded houses is actually a channel of grace.

Feast of the Holy Innocents (December 28)
(Mt 2:13–18)

The Feast of the Holy Innocents—which honors the children that King Herod, hoping to kill the Christ Child, executed en masse—is a deeply paradoxical saint's day. This is the feast of martyrs unaware of the existence of Christ, confessors unable to speak, saints of a Church of which they had never heard.

The basic problem is this: Herod's slaughter of the children of Bethlehem, by which he attempted to eliminate Jesus as a potential rival to the throne (Mt 2:13–18, today's first reading), is an appalling act of injustice. But suffering injustice does not by itself make a person a saint. Sanctity would seem to be the product of the will (in cooperation with grace); one becomes a saint by choosing God repeatedly and with deliberate intent throughout one's life. Today's liturgical prayers grapple with this difficulty: How could an infant possibly be a saint? The Prayer after Communion proclaims the Holy Innocents to be "Saints" who were "crowned with heavenly grace on account of his [Christ's] birth" but also admits they were "unable to profess your [God's] son in speech". Professing God's Son would seem to be a bare minimum prerequisite for Christian sainthood; the death of a person mentally unable to affirm belief in Christ would seem to be a misfortune, not a martyrdom.

Today we took our daughter to the zoo for the first time. Since it was thirty degrees outside and Beatrice is not yet two, we picked a tiny zoo where we could push her through on a stroller in about thirty minutes. Emily carefully bundled Beatrice up in a heavy pink parka with purple polka dots and took no end of photos (it is Emily's fate to be left out of most of our family photos, since she carefully chronicles our lives and I hate photography). The zoo possessed only a few exotic animals: a red panda (who refused to show his face), a leopard, a zebu, a marmoset, some monkeys, and a big lizard or two. Mostly, we strolled past relatively small American animals that to the adult mind didn't seem quite zooworthy: a turtle, an owl, some prairie dogs (prairie dogs?), a wolverine, a wolf. The toddler was impressed anyway. In photo after photo, her face points upward, eyes wide open; a rigid arm juts out of the stroller, saluting each new species. When we took her out of the stroller, lifted her up, and snapped her back into the car seat, we asked her what her favorite zoo animal was. "The woof!" she excitedly replied, without hesitation.

Herod killed all male children in Bethlehem under the age of two. My daughter is the same age they were. And she wishes she could hang out not with pandas, not with prairie dogs, not even with monkeys, but with *wolves*. Any child who thinks that wolves seem fun is in no position to choose martyrdom consciously. Toddlers aren't good enough at survival to be martyrs. The trick is—sometimes despite their best efforts—to keep them alive.

So how can the Holy Innocents be saints? The Collect suggests an answer: they "confessed and proclaimed" Almighty God "not by speaking but by dying". Somehow, in God's mercy, their actions had meaning beyond their stated intentions—or even their ability to state an intention. They were saints killed for the sake of Christ, although they lacked any intention at all. And the Church's message here may give all hope: we all need our lives and actions to possess meaning beyond our intentions.

For, really, how much of the good that gets done in the world happens as the result of a conscious, direct, perfect, and pure intention? The missionary movement, which spread the Faith to all parts of the earth, was one of the great developments in human history; Jesus' Great Commission to make disciples of all nations was taken seriously and in large part fulfilled (Mt 28:19–20). But even here, motives were mixed, as Catholicism was often spread by missionary priests sponsored by European governments as part of the project of imperial expansion. The great historical event of my lifetime has been the collapse of atheistic communism, which was inspired in part by Blessed John Paul II's heroic leadership and spiritual force.[2] Yet, the collapse of the Soviet Union was occasioned just as much by the country's impending economic bankruptcy—which was triggered by its inability to keep up with the fiscal demands of its arms race with the United States. And what saint, pope, or bishop cheered on the arms race? To switch to a more personal register, I'm a teacher, which is a rather idealistic profession. And I did go to graduate school partly because I wanted to help others by teaching them to write and to reason more effectively. But there is also a less noble angle: I desperately wanted to get out of the restaurant where I was working; I was tired of grease burns. In sum, if you take away all cases where a conscious, pure, and single motive is absent, precious little good is left in human history—and in my own biography.

The Feast of the Holy Innocents reminds us that, in a sense, we're all Holy Innocents, and our lives have

---

[2] When I composed this meditation, John Paul II was a blessed. He has since been canonized.

meaning, purpose, and even a kind of grandeur primarily because God takes us at more than our intention. In his time, in his pattern, in his light, in the liturgical year, even those events we suffered or bungled through without any conscious plan or design can receive a transcendent significance. As I look for meaning, pattern, and purpose in my life this year, the hope of the Holy Innocents must be mine as well.

Feast of the Holy Family (December 30) (Col 3:12–21)

Two days ago, my family traipsed through the zoo, taking pictures, smiling for the camera, and laughing loudly. We looked like we belonged in an unusually saccharine magazine advertisement. Today we appeared far less idyllic.

My wife works at a large university and spends the day shuffling from meeting to meeting on a moped because, as with all large universities, parking is impossible, and she can't otherwise get from building to building on time. Now, our city council, like Caesar Augustus, has passed a decree that all (that is, all mopeds) must be taxed (and plated). Of course, you can't drive the moped to city hall to get the license plate, because then you would be violating the law by operating an unregistered vehicle. So we ordered a cheap motorcycle carrier for the back of our Ford Escape and began the day trying to assemble it. Emily always prefers to tackle a job herself, so she did the bulk of the work while I made sure Beatrice didn't ingest anything that wasn't food. But Emily did ask me to finish up by tightening a couple of bolts.

Thirty minutes later, I was still spinning a socket wrench back and forth, frantically trying to tighten two bolts—which, alas, was a fairly predictable result. My father is a retired skilled tradesman (a machine repairman, an expert who fixes not merely automobiles but the assembly lines that build them), so I should know how to use a wrench. But even before my parents' divorce, he was typically absent from the family, and when present seemed in a chronic state of frustration and impatience; his few attempts to train me in matters mechanical went terribly awry. Even now, when I try to fix things or to assemble furniture, reason deserts me. I mix up my left and my right, alternate between tightening and loosening the same bolt, between turning the wrench so gently the bolt won't move and forcing the wrench so violently the bolt gets stripped, all in a crescendo of panic.

Emily threw open the door of the screen porch and saw me still desperately fiddling with the socket wrench. Her eyes widened, her head tilted slowly sideways, she stopped dead. She muttered, "Great. A meltdown. I never should have bought the stupid scooter," and she began bitterly wondering aloud whether—if we're too incompetent even to get it registered—we should just sell the thing. I hate to be chewed out but don't particularly blame her; my father, whatever his faults, was good at fixing things, and I often think that this is what fathers are for.

The story doesn't end all that badly. I called my mechanically inclined father-in-law, who came over and helped Emily finish assembling the motorcycle carrier, and we took the moped downtown and got it registered. I was asked to take on only one more task: to help unload the scooter from the carrier at the end of the day. I dropped the moped and scratched the finish. Still, the day ended with the scooter legal and basically intact and my wife and me on polite terms. Given the start, this was a comparative victory. Nothing was really damaged but my pride.

In this flutter of errands—some of which I've omitted— I didn't end up getting to look at the readings from the lectionary. So, as I sat down this evening with the lectionary, I couldn't imagine what the liturgical year could possibly have to say to me today of all days. And I found that it was the Feast of the Holy Family. Unlike Joseph (another skilled tradesman), I am no carpenter. But the epistle reading (Col 3:12–21) on forbearance is perfect for a typically muddled family like my own. The essence of a holy family is that its members "bear[ ] with one another and forgive[ ] one another" (13)—as my wife must (and did) my mechanical ineptitude and I must (and did) her temper—and this perhaps is what makes any family work. Jesus, though he was God, deferred to Joseph and Mary and bore with them. Mary, though she was sinless, submitted to Joseph. And, as the Gospel of Matthew suggests, though Joseph—neither divine nor immaculately conceived—seems to be the weak link in this chain, he was a just man, and this was enough to keep the Holy Family together.

Solemnity of Mary, Holy Mother of God (January 1) (Gal 4:4–7; Lk 2:16–21)

Today is what used to be called the Feast of the Circumcision, on which we celebrated Jesus' official induction into the Jewish community on the eighth day of his life. The readings still reflect the feast's origin, as the Gospel (Lk 2:16–21) narrates Jesus' circumcision and the epistle (Gal 4:4–7) explains how through Christ we ourselves receive adoption into God's family. As the new year begins, we celebrate Jesus' reception into the human family, his willingness to be subject to the ritual that established his identity as a Jewish male under covenant; by extension, we also celebrate Christ's willingness to experience the blessings and limitations of humanity and human identity, limitations he had to assume if we were to be redeemed. The title "Mother of God"—the assertion that Mary is the Theotokos, the God-bearer, the carrier of God in human form—is just another way of expressing that same basic mystery, though I may prefer the feast's older title.

None of us preexisted our human form, so none of us will ever know quite what it was like for Christ to learn the limits of material existence. But we all know to some degree what it means to be trained to be human. I watch my daughter as she begins to develop language. She is presently obsessed with trying to order the world through possessives. Everything belongs to somebody: there is "Mama chair, Daddy chair, Bea chair"; even the couch, where our spoiled dog lounges all day, is "dog chair". Besides learning the parts of speech, she is attempting to give the world a structure, trying to see how things fit together and interrelate. It's a paradox beyond comprehension that Christ, the Wisdom of God by whom all things were made, also learned to find a pattern in the world, a pattern that—as he intuitively recalled though he hadn't yet the words to express it—he himself put there. And, as he found the words, he would share them with us, and our redemption would begin.

January 4 (Weekdays of Christmas to the Epiphany) (Jn 1:35–42)

In today's Gospel (Jn 1:35–42), Jesus, just beginning his public ministry, calls Andrew to be an apostle. Andrew, a devout Jew, is already a disciple of John the Baptist. Andrew hears John proclaim Jesus to be "the Lamb of God", then leaves John to follow the Lamb (36–37). Andrew spends the day with Jesus, then goes back home to get his brother Simon, whom Jesus also embraces as an apostle and renames "Cephas" or Peter (41–42).

This Gospel grapples with a basic paradox about the nature of faith. Faith must always be an individual decision, but it cannot exist without community. Actually, for the most part, community precedes faith; we generally accept the Faith because we have first embraced the community of faith (and not vice versa). John the Baptist is the exception. He is a prophet. He can see Jesus for what he is (the Lamb of God) without the aid of any human intermediary; he realizes it by direct revelation from God. Andrew, by contrast, follows the rule. Like the rest of us, he sees no divine sign. But he is, as Scripture points out, already a "disciple" (37), already part of the community gathered around John the Baptist. When he first encounters Jesus, he knows nothing about him, but he *does* know plenty about John. He makes his initial decision to follow Christ based on his faith in John the Baptist; any relationship with or personal knowledge of Christ comes afterward.

So it is for many of us. I knew a girl who began to believe in Christ simply because the Evangelical Protestants in her high school were the only people who weren't jerks to her, and I knew of another who came to faith because the campus ministries at her public college were the only places where she could socialize with people who weren't drunk. These are both versions of Andrew's story: Andrew believes in Jesus because he trusts John the Baptist, and—at another level of remove—Peter believes because he trusts Andrew. The community comes first and meets our needs, appeals to us where we are.

And this is my story as well. By the time I was in high school, I had lost faith in the Pentecostal religion in which I was raised and had become an artsy teenage agnostic. I hated southern Michigan and read widely and randomly for both self-improvement and escape. In the books I read, I was primarily seeking artistic virtuosity and complexity of thought. I was an earnest, intellectually engaged, and probably insufferable teen. I was the sort of person who refused to tell restaurant patrons, "Have a nice day," on the grounds of insincerity (what does the phrase mean, anyway?) and objected to calling our specials "limited-time offers" on the grounds of redundancy (all time is, by nature, limited). I was the sort of person who becomes an English major.

But in the course of my reading I discovered that of all the authors I had encountered, Dante composed the best poetry, Augustine best penetrated the mysteries of the human psyche, Blaise Pascal best fathomed the nature of faith and doubt, and G. K. Chesterton told the funniest jokes. Each, to my surprise, was a Catholic, and as a group, they had only their Catholicism in common. So I started going to Mass. It would be accurate to say that at this point in my life I accepted the Catholic Church only because I believed in her literature, and believed in Jesus only because I believed in the Catholic Church. On one level, this whole procedure is profoundly backward and would appall any devout Catholic. Viewed another way, it is simply just and right. As Thomas Aquinas pointed out, God is the author of all good, and all goods in themselves draw us to God if we let them. Each of these authors in his wisdom discerned some part of the divine pattern; the literary by-products of the Catholic community pulled me back to Christ.

But that can never be the whole story. For all of us, I think, there is also a further point, where we must encounter Christ personally and respond to the challenge of his call. When Andrew walks up to Jesus, Jesus asks him to "come" and see where he is "staying" (Jn 1:39).

To remain in Christ is not to be stationary, and Andrew, to follow Jesus, has to leave even John the Baptist behind. Whatever brought us to the Faith serves only as a port of entry; it is not the entirety of the Faith. In my own case, I've had to realize that Catholicism is not primarily a literary movement or a philosophical system. The Catholic Church is a vast and dynamic institution almost as complex as humanity itself. As G. K. Chesterton said in his book of the same title, the Faith is not an idea but "the Thing"; it is not an abstraction but a way of life. Catholicism is lived daily by over a billion people, most of whom have no interest in literature or philosophy at all, and most of whom live better Catholic lives than mine.

Although I am fond of intellectually defending Catholicism, I find living that faith on a daily basis, connecting what I know with what I do, to be far more difficult. This is a journey I am still on, the inspiration in many ways for my liturgical year.

There is always another step to take; to believe is to be in motion.

2

WORKING FOR THE WEEKEND
(Ordinary Time, Round 1)

Tuesday of the First Week in Ordinary Time
(1 Sam 1:9–20; Mk 1:21–28)

For the next year, I'm in charge of the Accreditation Task Force for my university. You don't need to know the details or even what an Accreditation Task Force is. For all practical purposes, you can substitute any gigantic project you've been given at work without also being given the training or the authority you would need actually to get the job done. The salient fact here is that if I screw up this project, the university is in big trouble, and I'm not at all sure what I'm supposed to be doing or how to do it.

So this morning I had intense stomach cramps. I began sticking my head under sinks and into showers to see if our plumbing had a drip anywhere. As it turns out, we do have a dripping showerhead that will need repair, and I began brooding over this repair as a challenge to my manhood that I would doubtless fail. Finally, I pulled myself away from the plumbing, poured a cup of coffee into a travel mug, jumped into the car, and whipped out of the driveway, hurrying for the highway. As I merged onto the highway, the lid came off my travel mug, and I dumped a cup of coffee all over my khakis. I didn't have time to go back and get a new pair of pants. I just had to hope that the two browns more or less matched. And then I realized that in the course of half an hour I had hit each of three ways I tend to displace my fears about a stressful situation (stomach upset, household maintenance problem, spilled beverage). "Record time," I thought with bemusement as I headed down the highway on my way to work. "A new personal best."

I prayed the rosary as I drove, trying to force my thoughts into some kind of order and trying to dwell on something more significant than a dripping showerhead. My prayer wasn't particularly focused as I drove through the rolling hills of central Virginia. While my car covered the empty miles, my thoughts moved back and forth between legitimate meditations on the Sorrowful Mysteries and my mundane fears about plumbing and accreditation. I felt, as I always feel, a little weird about praying this way— driving distracted, unfocused, and minimally coherent, probably a road hazard—for surely God deserves better.

I took some comfort from the first reading for today (1 Sam 1:9–20), which I glanced over this morning just before I poured the cup of coffee I would later dump. We're back to the story of Hannah (see my December 22 entry). Now the focus of the reading is not her surrender of her son, Samuel, to God but her earlier prayer at the temple at Shiloh that she might bear a child in the first place. She prays in such an agitated and apparently incoherent manner—"weeping copiously" in "her bitterness" but uttering no clear words aloud—that Eli the priest thinks she must be drunk (10, 12–13). When Eli confronts her about her scandalous behavior (what could be more sacrilegious than being drunk in the temple itself?), she implores him to realize that her actions are prompted not by alcohol but instead "by deep sorrow and misery" (16). I probably also appeared drunk as I drove to work today—muttering to myself, drifting around the road, obviously distracted.

I strive for a highly rational faith, and distrust emotion. I believe in God. I like to draw lessons from the life of Christ and attempt to imitate him. But I disdain my own psychological weaknesses and tics. I find it difficult (as this morning) even to try to do what Hannah undoubtedly really did: give oneself over to God with all one's faults, without reservation, praying a prayer so devoid of self-composure or social pretense that it could actually appear mad. But if I can't do that, how can God transform and change me? Our "best self"—the rational, civil, kind, and self-controlled person we aspire to be—is only a small part of who we really are. Unless we will lay our whole selves open before God, holding nothing back, how can he move in our depths and—as in the Gospel reading (Mk 1:21–28)—cure us of the demons that plague our subconscious and that cannot be expunged by mere effort and will?

Thursday of the First Week in Ordinary Time
(1 Sam 4:1–11; Ps 44:10–11, 14–15, 24–25)

In today's first reading (1 Sam 4:1–11), the Israelites face a universal human question. Where is God when things aren't going well for us? How should we respond to defeat as individuals and as a nation?

The Israelites are (as always, it seems) fighting the Philistines. In their anxiety about the upcoming battle, in their time of crisis, they make what would appear to be the right decision. They rediscover their nation's religious traditions and spiritual heritage. Surely, they reason, the solution to their problems is the Ark of the Covenant: the sacred box containing the tablets of the Law that had accompanied them through the desert and into the Promised Land, the symbol of all they are as a people pledged to God. So they go into battle marching behind the Ark.

This seemingly fail-safe solution backfires badly. The Israelites lose the battle anyway, and, worse, the Philistines take the Ark as plunder. Prior to the battle, the downtrodden Israelites thought that God seemed absent and the divine message illegible; now he seems entirely gone. The symbol of his rule and his reign, the Ark, *is* entirely gone. Today's Responsorial Psalm (Ps 44:10–11, 14–15, 24–25) gives voice to this sort of anguish, lamenting that the Lord, who now seems to "hide [his] face" and "forget[ ]" his people, will "go not forth with our armies", leaving the people to be "plundered" and treated with "mockery and scorn" by the nations (25, 10–11, 14).

What are we to make of these sobering readings as we move into Ordinary Time? Perhaps that often when we look for a sign of God's action in the world and do not find it, it is because we are viewing the world in an egocentric way. The problem of evil—why God hides himself, why God allows suffering—is a legitimate theological issue. But it's not the starving children in Haiti who most often cause me to question the benevolence of God. I question God if things are going poorly for me at work, if there is tension at home, if appliances break, if my weaknesses are exposed and the good I do isn't rewarded.

I am writing at a corner desk in our compact upstairs study, one room over from the converted half bath that contains the prefab shower unit with the dripping head. I can hear it dripping as I write. I know that I will prove unable to fix it and that this lapse is going to make me feel like a failure as a husband and a man. So I stop writing and pray—first in the study in front of a three-inch porcelain statue of Mary that has accompanied me on every move for seventeen years, and then in the master bedroom in front of a crucifix that was blessed by a priest shortly after our wedding—that God would make it stop dripping. I honestly and earnestly pray this prayer, with more fervor than I muster when praying for the poor or for an end to abortion. Of course, the problem here isn't really the showerhead (and this really is no crisis; I can—and after a few failures, shortly will—just call a plumber). The problem is that in some ways I've misdefined what it means to be a man. I don't greatly value the abilities God has given me, and I overly esteem those I do not possess. A miraculous intervention to stop the drip would just confirm me in the ways in which I falsely define myself and the world. It would do my soul less than no good. God intervenes in my life by failing to grant my prayer.

We need to be reminded that God is transcendent and that sometimes we can learn only through defeat. The Ark, most scholars believe, is here being used by the Israelites as a kind of magical fetish. The Israelites think that the Ark itself will deliver them through its divine power. They are venerating the symbolic object but ignoring what it signifies; they make no attempt to follow the Ark's internal contents, the tablets of the Law. By allowing the Ark to be captured, God shows that he will not be treated in this manner. Similarly, we can—and I did today—pray in front of a crucifix, begging that our desires would be fulfilled and our fears averted, forgetting that the Cross itself teaches us that getting what we want is not the way to God.

Wednesday of the Second Week in Ordinary Time
(1 Sam 17:32–33, 37, 40–51)

Today's first reading (1 Sam 17:32–33, 37, 40–51) is the "David and Goliath" narrative, a story so famous that it has passed into cliché. Of course, I've heard this story thousands of times, and I regularly read it to my daughter in her children's Bible. But one moment in the story suddenly stands out as if I had never read it before. The teenage shepherd David is the only person in the Israelite army willing to take on the battle-seasoned warrior and literal giant Goliath. No one else is applying for the job, but King Saul still has his reservations. Saul tells David that a "youth" like him cannot really fight a Philistine who "has been a warrior from his youth" (33). David replies, "The Lord, who delivered me from the claws of the lion and the bear [during David's employment as a shepherd], will also keep me safe from the clutches of this Philistine" (37).

Perhaps I am being too much the English teacher here, but I wonder if the three theological virtues (faith, hope, and charity) could be understood in terms of the three basic verb tenses (past, future, and present). Hope as a virtue may be oriented toward the future; faith may be oriented more toward the past and present, as it interprets the meaning of both past experience and the world we presently inhabit. David has seen the divine hand at work in his life in childhood, and this has given him full confidence that God will accompany him in the very different circumstances of adulthood; his faith has given him hope.

I have trouble making this move from faith to hope. I do ponder over, and am grateful for, the ways in which God has provided for me in the past. How I managed to pay for my own undergraduate education, obtain full funding for graduate school, and land a permanent job in an enormously glutted field remain mysteries to me inexplicable except for the operation of grace. When all indicators suggested I would not be going to graduate school, I lit a candle and prayed in front of a statue of Mary and asked her to intercede for me, trusting she could pray with purer motives than I could muster. Three days later, I was accepted with funding at Ohio State. When the job market seemed impossible, I entered a period of fasting and prayer; a few days later, papers were signed, and I found myself on the way to teaching at a small public teachers college. God has had a hand in whatever has gone well in my life, and that hand has often been displayed in a surprisingly open manner.

But I have difficulty learning from my past experiences with God. I tend to think of the future in terms of disruption or discontinuity. Actually, since the circumstances of life are continually changing, I have trouble applying *anything* from my past to my future. What does a hyperactive five-year-old spinning in circles have to do with a sullen teenager writing poetry in graveyards, a cynical twenty-something fast-food employee placating an irate customer, or a thirty-nine-year-old professor grading papers? These people have nothing to say to each other, even if they are all me. Right now I'm in a flat panic about having to handle the central part of my college's reaccreditation project, and my past experiences don't particularly help. The cynical fast-food employee just glares at college professors, the sullen teen says, "We're all going to die someday anyway, so what does it matter?" and the hyperactive five-year-old just keeps kicking all of us in the shins.

But what David has learned is not so much his own nature—which he frequently calls a "mystery" in the Psalms—as the nature of God. He does not offer a detailed résumé-style argument as to how the skills of his previous position as a shepherd are applicable to his desired position as a warrior. He says that over the course of his life he has learned something about the character of God and thus something about the nature of the universe in which he lives. Through hard experience, David has come to realize that God can be trusted. David can throw himself into a series of impossibly difficult situations not because he has a tremendous amount of self-confidence but because he realizes the outcome is out of his hands and is, in fact, in better hands than his own. He is an analyst not of his own character but of God's.

Friday of the Second Week in Ordinary Time (1 Sam 24:3–21)

In the first reading for today (1 Sam 24:3–21), King Saul is attempting to kill David as a possible rival for his throne, and David has gone into hiding. During his pursuit of David, Saul realizes that he needs to relieve himself and enters a cave (the ancient Israelites considered caves to be nature's outhouses) (4). As fate would have it, Saul enters the very cave where David and his men have already hidden to conceal themselves from Saul's troops. David now has the perfect opportunity to kill Saul—he has him literally with his pants down, as David's men point out. But David lets Saul go, merely cutting off part of his robe to serve as proof that the event actually happened.

Although I am by birth and breeding a Midwesterner, I now live in the South. I'm not sure if the South is more Christian than the rest of the nation in practice, but certainly it is more Christian in its speech patterns. Religious phraseology drips off Southern lips as inevitably as sweat from Southern pores. On the whole, I rather like this; it's a refreshing change from the rapid secularization of culture that has otherwise been my adult experience. One ubiquitous phrase, however, is the bane of my Southern existence: "Everything happens for a reason." I've heard this phrase on the lips of everyone from elderly

Fundamentalist real estate agents to trendy twentysomething lesbians (real examples).

My biggest problem with the phrase is its upbeat fatal-
ism. One fundamental lesson of the fall of man is that we
live in a world where things often happen for no particular reason; once evil and suffering are introduced into
the world, their ultimate effects can't be charted on a simple line graph. Part of my Catholic faith is that, while *some*
things happen for a reason (we do not live in a nihilistic
universe; there is such a thing as causality), many things *do*
happen for no reason at all. I have enough faith to reject
the pious Southern cliché.

The other problem with this phrase, however, is that
it simply equates the workings of chance or fortune with
the will of God. This is a human tendency to which we
all—including me—are prone. When circumstances come
together to make everything work out for us, we determine we must be seeing the will of God in action. This is
precisely the view of David's men when Saul stumbles into
exactly the wrong cave. "The Lord," they say, was obviously "deliver[ing]" Saul into David's "grasp" and would
want him to take advantage of the situation (1 Sam 24:5).
My wife and I are again discussing whether we should
leave our relatively modest first home for a larger home
in a better neighborhood (or, rather, my wife is discussing
this topic, and since she usually turns out to be right, I'm
listening with as open a mind as I can manage). As far
as our Southern friends and neighbors are concerned, the
answer to the question is obvious: we've been blessed with
promotions at work, so God must want us to move somewhere upscale. Everything happens for a reason.

On the other hand, when circumstances conspire to
thwart our desires, we feel that what we wanted must
not have been God's will for us after all; we must have

misunderstood his will. Sometimes this conclusion is perfectly true. Sometimes God mercifully thwarts our plans because we're being fools and need to be stopped before we damage ourselves and others. But taken as an absolute principle, this idea confuses luck with holiness. My sister, who is smart, sardonic, and capable and has a college degree, has been able to find nothing better than part-time work for two years. "What's the reason?" my Southern friends would wonder. In this case, the reason—she lives in metro Detroit, which leads the nation in unemployment— is easy to identify but not very spiritually enlightening. And this kind of reasoning leaves no room for the Cross. *Because* Jesus did exactly what was right, all the pieces fell precisely in line—for him to be crucified.

I'm like anybody else. I hate failure and love success and tend to equate my patterns of successes and failures with the voice of God saying yes or no. But David is wiser. If everything does happen for a reason (which is itself doubtful), the reason must often be one far from obvious. David distrusts his happy chance and sees the situation as a moral test, one that he passes by refraining from killing Saul— and it is this restraint that in God's eyes ultimately makes him fit to be king. He won't "lay a hand" on "the Lord's anointed" (1 Sam 24:7). The circumstance becomes a defining moment for David—only because he didn't allow circumstance to dictate his view of God but allowed God to dictate his view of circumstance.

Saturday of the Second Week in Ordinary Time
(Mk 3:20–21)

Today's Gospel (Mk 3:20–21) is short but disturbing. Jesus' relatives witness his outlandish pronouncements and his huge crowds of ragtag and disreputable followers, and they decide he must be insane. "He is out of his mind," they exclaim (3:21). Basically, Jesus' relations are respectable, hardworking blue-collar guys, and they're telling the renegade carpenter—in their eyes, perhaps, the guy who's too lazy to do his proper job—to drop the prophet business, settle down, and build some tables. Would-be prophets are a dime a dozen. Well-built tables are hard to find. And life must go on.

It's easy to tell when someone has deviated from the norm. Even in a crowd, we notice instinctively the man picking his nose or the woman stifling tears. How we respond to deviation from the social norm is often less a matter of spiritual discernment and more a matter of upbringing. For solid Midwestern middle-class citizenry, like my wife's family, deviation from the norm is a matter of abhorrence; "Well, they're not exactly normal" is as extreme a pronouncement of condemnation as my in-laws possess. Evangelical Protestants, they even spent most of their lives in a denomination called the *Regular* Baptist church. What "regular" was originally intended to mean in this theological context, I do not know, but in point of practice the church does seem to worship and enforce regularity. It is a congregation of hardworking, well-meaning engineers and small businessmen and their wives, all clad in subdued formal wear; apart from faith, it could be (in the best and worse senses) any small town service organization.

On the other hand, I was raised by Pentecostal ex-hippies and received my early religious training at a hard-rock, storefront church where everything was in earth tones and everyone wore fringe. As far as we were concerned, people who followed social norms were obviously far from God—they were "Pharisees" seeking their salvation in money, status, or man-made religion. Anyone who radically violated expected standards of behavior was probably inspired by God. And at times, this proved true, as hopeless drug addicts had their lives turned around at church services raucous enough to result in neighboring businesses and homeowners calling the police. One of my earliest memories is of hippies with their arms locked together dancing in a chain through the church, out the door, around the building, and back again, amplifiers blaring, Jesus rock and tongue-speaking filling the night air—until the cops came and broke up the gathering.

In my early twenties, I fell briefly in love with a radical feminist high school teacher, who was the unconventional type of person my upbringing had prepared me (unintentionally) to fall for. She lived with her enormous dog in a tiny apartment where she wrote poetry, read volumes of feminist literary theory, and listened to alternative rock. She was blunt, sarcastic, and forceful; a military college graduate, she once threw me on her back and carried me to safety after I had an asthma attack during what was supposed to be a romantic moonlit walk on a beach. She enjoyed this reversal of gender roles; I merely appreciated being able to breathe again.

Several months later, as I sat reading in a beige cloth recliner in her apartment, she threw a shelf's worth of books at my head, slowly and deliberately, reading the titles aloud and commenting on them as she did so. As I ducked the flying books and backed away from her growling dog, I began to I realize that one may violate a social norm in three very different ways:

1. by transcending the norm in light of a higher standard or higher insight (as do Jesus and the saints),

2. by falling below the norm and failing to live up to the basic standards of decency that it provides (as do criminals and the simply amoral), or

3. by thrashing about the norm, behaving according to no consistent standard.

(The present instance, I now thought, was a case of number 3 passing for number 1.)

We can fall into delusion and miss the voice of God by following radical, transgressive figures (who often aren't shy about calling themselves prophets); we can do the same thing by following safe, respectable figures (who may even be priests). Liberals go one way, conservatives the other, but we may both be lost.

This dilemma seems to present itself especially when it comes to the question of basic lifestyle matters—such as, at present, whether and where our three-person family should move. We want to make a decision informed by our faith. Our Christian conservative friends say, "You've got a child now. Your first duty is to your family. For her sake, you've got to live in as safe [read: rich] a neighborhood as possible." Our Christian radical friends say, "Buy a beat-up old Victorian house downtown and fix it up. Live near [read: not with] Christ's poor." Basically, "Be respectable", like my wife's family; or, "Be bohemian", like, historically, my own. Same old questions, same old answers, none particularly spiritually informative.

We need to know where God may be leading us, and often that voice comes to us through other people. So where do you find the voice of God if you can trust neither conformity nor nonconformity? How in cases like this does one discern the divine call from its counterfeits?

I am no longer sure I know. I do know that the Church thinks more deeply and perceptively than I; I hope that this year of living liturgically, of thinking with the Church, will lead me to an answer more legitimate than these reflex reactions, to some kind of real wisdom.

Conversion of Saint Paul the Apostle (January 25) (Acts 22:3–16)

Today is the Feast of the Conversion of Saint Paul. I have trouble celebrating this feast, since as a child I was abused by the conversion of Saint Paul. As I've mentioned, I grew up as a Pentecostal. The crisis conversion constituted our entire model of the spiritual life. There is a good side to this model—we held out hope for everyone, regardless of how improbable it seemed at the moment that his life story could have a happy ending. And sometimes the crisis conversion happened—the drug addict put down the Bible whose pages he had been systematically tearing off, chewing, and swallowing, and walked off a sane man (true story); the black-clad teenager who had attempted suicide multiple times suddenly saw a purpose in life and had the courage to get out of bed.

But often, the crisis conversion ended up being a cudgel with which unemotional people like me were regularly beaten. Since we held that you could possess a saving relationship with God only if you had had a crisis conversion—a specific, definable moment at a particular date, in which you renounced evil and chose Christ, and after which your life changed in specific, documentable ways—we all felt a tremendous pressure to produce one. Middle-aged men raised in the church told absurd stories of what evil three-year-olds they had been before their professions of faith and what righteous three-year-olds they had been thereafter. I thought that the unacknowledged real meaning of their stories was simply that at one time, they had been three years old; three-year-olds act at random, seeming children of heaven or hell at any given moment.

At one church I attended, we were literally locked in each Sunday until a given number of people—a variable figure set spontaneously each week by the pastor and, putatively, the Holy Spirit—had come to the altar to experience a crisis conversion. I came to recognize the signs that the altar call was approaching: the preacher's voice ceasing its shouting and suddenly becoming low and intimate; the musicians shifting in their seats, knowing that they would soon be called up to provide mood music; the men in the sound booth adjusting for the final number. And, seeing the signs, I would slip out just before the ushers physically barred the doors, then hide until the conclusion of the service reading books in a bathroom stall. Our church's approach to faith did much for my literary knowledge; it did not do much for my relationship with God. And, invariably, the Bible story that was told to justify this approach was the conversion of Saint Paul, knocked down and blinded just as he was on his way to butcher the early Church, and thereafter her greatest missionary, a crisis conversion if there ever was one.

I'm not temperamentally dramatic. I'm skeptical and quizzical and make large decisions very slowly. In the tradition in which I was raised, it would be a fair question whether a person like me could have a relationship with God at all. My reserve and caution could be, and often were, taken to indicate a lack of feeling for the deity, a blasé attitude incommensurate with redemption. One of the great reliefs for me of converting to Catholicism—a process that, characteristically, spanned two periods of my life, starting in high school and ending in college—was that I thought no one would ever again ask me when I "got saved". I thought I had left crisis conversion behind forever. But here we are at the Conversion of Saint Paul, and the first reading (Acts 22:3–16) recounts this most famous of all crisis conversions.

An unfortunate consequence of my reaction against crisis conversion is that I tend to discount the possibility of people altering at all. I tend to assume that everyone will simply remain as he is and seemingly always has been. If you're betting on someone changing his life, you're always betting against the odds (as the vast number of relapses after crisis conversions that I saw growing up would attest; the drug addict miraculously delivered often later returns to the pleasures and pains he had left behind, and the perpetually suicidal teen tries again). Hence, if I see a sudden and dramatic conversion—even to Catholicism—I'm immediately, and perhaps uncharitably, skeptical. And this skepticism extends even to my own attempts to change and grow closer to God. Throughout this year, I've been haunted by a nagging sense that the quest to live my life in light of the liturgy is futile, because regardless of what I do, I will always remain exactly as I am, with the same main virtues and the same besetting sins.

But the whole idea of Christianity, in many ways, is that—while it need not occur at a single moment of crisis— we *can* be transformed, remade in Christ. And transformations *do* happen; faith isn't a question of playing the numbers or of running the statistical odds. The wisdom of the Church can be seen in that, while she knows better than to define crisis as the normal means of conversion, she also won't let us forget about or give up on conversion altogether. So it turns out that I do need this feast, which I would really rather avoid. The Conversion of Saint Paul can remind me this year to be open to the possibility of conversion, in myself and in others, when-ever and however it occurs.

Fourth Sunday in Ordinary Time (1 Cor 7:32–35)

Last night I drove two hours and fifteen minutes up to the farthest southern exurb of Washington, D.C., to eat din-ner at Chili's, an anonymous casual dining place that you can find in any decent-sized town. I do this once or twice a year to meet up with an old friend from graduate school. She is a tall, carefully put-together brunette from the New York City suburbs who holds a Ph.D. in mathematics and does research work in physics for one of the biggest labs in the country. She is perceptive, self-deprecating, well-read, and a good conversationalist. And by most standards, she is well-off. But increasingly our conversations turn on what it's like for her to be nearing the age of forty single. Her fate always strikes me as an argument against Darwinian evolution. If the species actually had any interest in its own betterment, she would have nine kids.

After dinner last night we sat in the Starbucks across the parking lot from Chili's—this city is replete with all the standard chains and not much else—discussing the biblical passage that bizarrely turns out to be the epistle reading for today (1 Cor 7:32–35). My friend was complaining that the married people so dominant in church life (especially in the Evangelical Protestant churches she attends) dismiss the complexities and difficulties of the single life by refer-encing this passage: "An unmarried woman or a virgin is anxious about the things of the Lord, so that she may be holy in both body and spirit. A married woman, on the other hand, is anxious about the things of this world, how she may please her husband" (34).

Others at church frequently tell my friend, "Isn't it wonderful that you have all this free time to serve the Lord? The church is your family."

"The church," she wryly observes, "isn't willing to come over and clean up my cat's vomit at two o'clock in the morning. A husband might get up and do it." And since she works over sixty hours a week, every week, she also doesn't have the time on her hands to perform vast acts of service to the church—"or the inclination", she admits candidly. "The single life means it's all on you. I can feel good about my accomplishments in life and the life I've made, but I'm the one who has made it. I've got no one to blame it on and no one to share it with."

I don't know what to say, so I respond flippantly that one of the great things about marriage is always having someone to blame your failures on. I don't know any married people, I reply, who weren't going to be a world-class, earth-changing something or other except that they nobly gave it up for their spouse. Now, if the world actually contained that many world-changing people, civilization would collapse into a perpetual state of chaos and the world would explode; humanity can handle only so much change, so rapidly. It's just as well that we all have limits. But being married, I've long said, means never having to acknowledge your own human limits; you've always got a scapegoat.

More seriously, I also admit that I don't recognize myself in the biblical ideal of marriage any more than my friend recognizes herself in the biblical ideal of singleness. You're supposed to be one flesh; but of course, like everyone else, Emily and I are always tugging in different directions, and our "one flesh" staggers along like kids in a three-legged race on field day.

So what do you do, my friend and I asked each other, when you recognize and are inspired by a biblical ideal but feel not only that you aren't there but that you have no meaningful connection to it? We sat in silence for a bit. It's strange to reach this level of honesty while sitting on fake leather chairs, sipping chai tea lattes made from some weird concentrate, and listening to a corporate soundtrack in one of the most anonymous cities in America. So we sipped our lattes and thought.

Finally I suggested that perhaps faith at least helps us know where true north is, so we can steer ourselves in more or less the right direction, however impossible or impassible our ultimate destination may seem to us at the moment. The three-legged race can keep hopping up the road. Then we realized it was late, got back in our cars, and leaving the exurb behind, drove our opposite ways into the night.

Saturday of the Fourth Week in Ordinary Time
(1 Kings 3:4–13)

Solomon's prayer upon becoming king (1 Kings 3:4–13, today's first reading) is a frank confession that he has no idea what he's doing: "I am a mere youth, not knowing at all how to act" (7).

He is off to a good start as king already. Many times I've sat in my office with an aspiring high school English teacher who is feeling discouraged because of a practicum with an abusive teacher or a student-teaching experience with a rough and rowdy class.

"I stink," she'll say, flipping her hair into her face, grabbing the plastic arms of the chair tightly, and looking down at her feet. "I'm never gonna make it. I've gotta get a new major."

"I *know* you'll be a great teacher one day," I reply.

"Quit it," she mumbles through her hair without looking up. "You're just being nice. Thanks—but quit it."

"No, really. I'm not that nice. I won't just say things."

She finally raises her head halfway, simply because with her head down she can't roll her eyes to any effect. "Okay, then," she asks, "why do you *think* I'm going to make it when I *know* I stink?"

"*Because* you think you stink. That means you're capable of realizing when things aren't going well. You can size up other people accurately. You know when you're losing a class and boring it to death. If you know when students are with you and when they're not, you'll eventually figure out how to keep them with you most of the time. Truly terrible teachers are so in love with their own voice that they've got no clue when they've lost the class. Think of the worst teacher you ever had. You know it's true."

I'm far from infallible, but I have yet to misadvise a student in this particular situation. And apparently my practical experience accords with God's judgment. Solomon—unlike his power-mad half-brothers Absalom and Adonijah—realizes that he has no idea how to be king. And God doesn't respond by giving him a lecture on the value of self-esteem; instead, he commends Solomon's accurate self-appraisal. "You're so right," says God. "You truly haven't a clue what you're doing! Glad you said it, not I."

Solomon is the Bible's most famous wisdom figure, and his story suggests that this sort of self-honesty is the basic preamble to wisdom. Practically, we can get better at anything only if we realize what we don't know. Ethically, we can help others only if we've overcome our ego enough to realize that they aren't us. Spiritually, we can move toward God only if we know in what respects we're far from him. "Know yourself," Socrates said, and if the news isn't always good, we have to be humble enough to take it. There is no other way to advance, spiritually or temporally.

I can only hope that this principle also applies in my own case. I'm two months into trying to live my life in light of the liturgy, and I have no idea what I'm doing or whether I've gotten anywhere. These ruminations record more failures to perceive God than brilliant moments of spiritual illumination. I'm no youth, but I still don't know "at all how to act". But I have admitted the disconnect I feel between my faith and my daily life, and that's some basic self-knowledge at least. The liturgical calendar is the ordinary means the Church employs to connect the glories of eternity with the mundane matters of daily life; a little of this sense of connection should rub off on me if I just stick close enough to the liturgical calendar for long enough.

Fifth Sunday in Ordinary Time (Job 7:1–4, 6–7; Ps 147:1–2, 3–4, 5–6)

If Solomon admits with me that he doesn't know what he is doing, Job today (7:1–4, 6–7, first reading) gives voice to my frequent sense that daily life is trivial and pointless. He rhetorically asks, "Is not man's life on earth a drudgery? Are not his days those of hirelings? He is a slave who longs for the shade" (1–2). In other words, man is a drone caught in a dead-end job of an existence, and he has only the quitting time of death to look forward to. So, as Job laments, he spends each moment of his life just waiting for that moment to pass. "If in bed, I say, 'When shall I arise?' then the night drags on" (4).

This hits home. I tend to spend my life hollowing out the present moment. I've always been this way. In high school, I looked down on my life and on those around me, imagining that college would be a perfect world devoid of drudgery and tedium. In college, I endured the restaurants where I worked by imagining how much better graduate school would be. In graduate school, I thought everything would have substance and meaning if I could just get out, get married, and have a family and a job. A sense of purpose was always deferred.

And now ... As I admitted at the beginning of this liturgical year, I'm the guy who sits in a coffee shop feeding his daughter a croissant so that he can work. I'm as absent from the moment as ever. I've merely changed the tactics by which I render my daily life devoid of meaning. Now that my life is a giant list of tasks on my office calendar, I evaporate the present moment by always focusing on the next task. As I talk on the phone to my family in Michigan (often about quite real and pressing family crises), I am both washing the turkey roaster in the sink and thinking about the composition papers I have to grade when I hang up; I'm not mentally present to the person with whom I'm speaking. As I grade papers and conference with students, I'm mentally drawing up a lesson plan for the next day's class. And so on. I'm never really there. Some spiritual writers discuss "the sacrament of the present moment". This is one sacrament that I have never received.

It's some consolation to see the Scripture readings explicitly grappling with this issue in the middle of the liturgical year. Job expresses the experience of all of us who have lived in unredeemed time, time as a sequence devoid of meaning, conducted according to the cadence of the time clock. Everyone is waiting for the next moment; everyone is waiting to punch out. In the words of a hit

song by the 1980s band Loverboy, "Everybody's working for the weekend", which is to say that we spend the
majority of life just killing time. Job reveals the dark truth
under this innocuous phrase; everyone working for the
weekend is unconsciously longing for death, the ultimate
clocking out. Sigmund Freud—who proclaimed in *Beyond
the Pleasure Principle* that "the aim of all life is death"—
couldn't have put it more starkly.

My worst days prove Job right. As I drive around the
bend on the local highway that serves as both the formal
entrance to the county where I work and a pickup site for
the county dump, I find myself thinking that if I just had a
sudden heart attack, all the deadlines I face for filing tech-
nical documents to help my college keep its accreditation
would become someone else's problem. Job in his relent-
less honesty reveals why one approaches life and time this
way: one's "days ... come to an end without hope" (Job
7:6). The empty march of time—the succession of tasks,
the minutes checked off on a time clock—is the chrono-
logical expression of despair.

The liturgical year expresses the opposite vision: the
saints' insight into life and time, the vision of those who
(like the author of Psalm 147, today's Responsorial Psalm
[vv. 1–2, 3–4, 5–6]) saw a pattern in their pain (the exile)
and a meaning in their joy (the restoration). This year, I'm
trying to work their liturgical equation backward, beginning with the saints' conclusions about time and hoping
in the end to see my life differently. In high school, I was
a big fan of the math textbooks that provided answers at
the back of the book (generally for odd problems only).
Usually if I could start with the conclusion, I could work
my way back to the premise. Then a concept that had
simply befuddled me—like so much of geometry—would
suddenly become clear. I'm hoping that this method still
does the trick.

Saturday of the Fifth Week in Ordinary Time
(1 Kings 12:26–32; 13:33–34)

The first reading today (1 Kings 12:26–32; 13:33–34) discusses how, following the split between the northern kingdom of Israel and the southern kingdom of Judah, the northern kingdom comes to worship not the uncreated God but a golden calf. Scripture is explicit about the essentially political origins of this religious decision. The golden calf was erected so that the people of Israel (in the north) wouldn't have to go to the temple in Jerusalem (in the south) to sacrifice; if the temple in Jerusalem remained the northern kingdom's spiritual authority, the king in Jerusalem would probably again become its political authority (12:26–27). So the northern king Jeroboam, although he certainly knows better after all his dealings with God's prophets, consolidates his political power by cynically creating a religious system in which he does not personally believe. He is, essentially, Henry VIII, who never really quit believing in Catholicism but created his own church anyway since he believed in his own power more. I wish atheist critics of the Bible would grapple with passages like this. There is nothing in Nietzsche's critique of religion as a mask for power that isn't already in 1 Kings. And 1 Kings is more nuanced and insightful than Nietzsche. To say that faith can be a structure manipulated by power (which is obviously true) is not to say that faith *must* be, and to say that it *must* be is as gross a distortion of history as saying that *all* faith of *any* sort is always ennobling.

So it's a fascinating scriptural moment—and the consciously duplicitous Jeroboam is an intriguing character, but one with whom it's hard to have much sympathy. I do have sympathy, though, for the people of Israel in the generations after Jeroboam, those who inherit the worship of the golden calf as a thing established. To worship the golden calf is not a decision they've ever consciously made. They are ignorant of the golden calf's origin as a manipulative political stunt (the author of 1 Kings writes from the southern kingdom). For them, the golden calf is God, and its worship is both piety and patriotism. To reject it is (it would seem) to be a traitor to their home, family, and government. The sins of the past become the next generation's assumed reality.

To give a more personal example, my mother left the Catholic Church long before I was born. As her high school graduation approached, she found that she was pregnant with my older brother. Her boyfriend agreed to marry her and had a job waiting in the factory that could provide for the family (a common tale of the times; think Bruce Springsteen's song "The River"). But, already an antiestablishment iconoclast (though the hippie phase and the Pentecostal conversion were both yet to come), he refused to be married in the Catholic Church. "I won't have my kids raised by the Pope!" he bluntly proclaimed.

My mother returned to the Church thirty years later, after my own conversion, and is a model of faith and prayerful devotion. But throughout my childhood, she was rabidly anti-Catholic. Catholics were legalists, Pharisees, formalists ignorant of both the Bible and the workings of the Spirit. Psychologically, her response was entirely understandable; she was filled with an unacknowledged sense of guilt over the faith she had abandoned, and unconsciously sought to settle the score with the Church that had raised her. I grew up saying that Catholics as a group were "idol worshippers" who were "spiritually dead". But when I spoke these phrases, I wasn't so much articulating a theological proposition as saying, "I love you, Mom."

On a national scale, over the last two decades the United States has begun to define "tolerance" and "diversity" as its central values. Many a public school teaches that

Christianity in general—and Catholicism in particular—is a bigoted faith that opposes these national values. Plenty of professors at my own college push this line, and grade accordingly. For the students who accept such teaching uncritically, patriotism requires a rejection of the Faith, and to embrace the Faith is to be un-American. This is their generation's assumed reality.

It's hard to see how one breaks this kind of cycle. Breaking through a kind of cultural feedback loop, in which the sins of one generation create the assumed reality of the next, may require a messenger from outside the culture, someone who challenges our automatic assumptions and perceptions. In the Bible, the worship of the golden calf was most often challenged by prophets from the southern kingdom who (like Amos) risked their lives by taking their messages north. Personally, I ran across a bunch of books by Catholic authors from other places, other times; as a teenager, I found their exoticism appealing. Perhaps the African and Asian priests presently coming in large numbers to North America to evangelize both the Roman Catholic Church and the Anglican Communion will prove to be these messengers for us and break us out of our feedback loop, teaching us to see the world anew.

Saturday of the Sixth Week in Ordinary Time
(Mk 9:2–13)

The Gospel today (Mk 9:2–13) relates the Transfiguration, Jesus' revealing of his true nature to his three chosen disciples, with Moses and Elijah miraculously present to attest that the Law and the prophets spoke to the same reality. This is one of the crucial moments in the Gospel, a verification that the *eschaton*, the end of the age, has already begun and that Jesus has always been who he is now. He doesn't become divine with the Baptism in the Jordan or the Resurrection. He has always been divine.

Jesus has always been divine, but he passed through the world unrecognized, which is scary to think about. We have to ask ourselves whether we have sufficient perception to recognize the divine when it stands in front of us. And for the most part, of course, we don't. It's not an easy thing to learn to comprehend divinity. Within the circle of the apostles, Jesus considers only three to be ready to encounter his Transfiguration. Even divine signs require interpretation, and a skeptic can always come up with some alternate explanation for the event; confronted directly with a miracle, a skeptic would still misread the signs. Our standards of proof assume an ordinary world operating in an ordinary way. How do you discern the divine or prove the seemingly impossible?

Yesterday, I got together with an old friend from Michigan who has now become a successful and deeply eccentric opera singer. We met in our teens; he is now in his midthirties and graying. He stands a head taller than me and carries himself with the grand gestures of a bass-baritone—projecting his voice and waving his arms wildly—even when walking down the street. He is an ex-Presbyterian who simultaneously flirts with the supernatural on its oddest occult fringes and mocks all the New Age superstitions in which he participates. He once dragged me into a New Age bookstore that reeked with incense. After purchasing the book on reincarnation he was looking for, he sarcastically bellowed in that quiet and dimly lit room, "Chene, how can you doubt the spiritual power of the good people who run this store? You can even *smell* the mysticism in here." The "good people" looked up and glared, offended and confused.

Yesterday, he told me that one of his music students, an ex-nun whom he was helping "get up the nun song for her nun reunion with her old order", recently prophesied to him during a lesson, "The universe is telling you to be free."

"Isn't that beautiful?" he added. "She's a lovely woman." Not thirty seconds later, he is telling me, "At the end of one lesson, she stopped in the doorway as she was leaving, extended her arms, and proclaimed, 'I created you.' I said, 'I've enjoyed working with you too.' What do you say to that? I didn't even realize until later that she was claiming that as a spiritual force she *had* ordered my creation and called me into being so I could eventually become her music teacher."

"Like Gnostic emanations," I suggested, "caught in some kind of mystical feedback loop."

"Exactly," he cheerfully agreed.

My friend is in his own way impossible to believe, particularly as a kid from the Detroit area and particularly as a friend of mine from back when I largely knew only people working in restaurants. Meeting him is obviously a very different occurrence from the Transfiguration. But it got me thinking about the insufficiency of material evidence to prove anything about humanity. We so much exceed our material traces. We leave the imprint of our person on those with whom we come into touch, but what's the physical or forensic trace? We've been taught to seek verification only through direct physical evidence, but this method leaves so much out.

If Peter, James, and John were to try to offer a physical proof of the Transfiguration, what could they provide? They could show the footprints on the mountain and the place where Peter wanted to build a tent. But how could they prove that the footprints were those of Moses and

Elijah, assuming that they left footprints at all? There is a kind of material trace, but it can't capture the force of spiritual presence.

To use a less miraculous analogy, I saw my opera friend for a few hours last night, but what proof do I now have of my encounter with such a character? An opera ticket—but anyone can get one of those. One of the few remaining signs of my friend's Midwestern origins is his passionate hatred of waste. Each of the rare times he blows into our area, he has insisted on giving away prior to his departure whatever he has purchased to keep himself comfortable during his rehearsal and performance at this particular venue. Once, it was an air purifier. Yesterday, it was partially finished bottles of ketchup and mustard, an onion, and a bunch of garlic. This is the only physical proof I have of my first encounter in years with one of the most charismatic people I've ever known. It's as insufficient as the footprints of the Transfiguration.

The evidence of human contact is human transformation, *ethos* (character) even more than *logos* (formal logic or proof). Aristotle says as much. The proof of Christ's Transfiguration is the character of the apostles, themselves transfigured by the character of Christ. The proof of the character of the apostles is the character of the Church they founded, and which persists to this day. The proof of Christ is the Church.

3

RENEW MY HEART, O GOD—
IF YOU MUST
(Lent and Holy Week)

Saturday after Ash Wednesday (Is 58:9b–14)

We often conceive what it means to be a Christian in America today in terms of the divide between conservative and liberal. Conservatives, it is thought, stand for personal holiness, while liberals stand for a just society (the "Social Gospel"); conservatives seek individual salvation, while liberals stand for the collective salvation of the social order; conservatives are concerned with purity (of rite, of theology, etc.), while liberals are concerned with charity. This divide is perpetuated even in how we carry out Lent. Conservatives stress the traditional personal disciplines of Lent, ascetically giving something up for the sake of the Gospel. By contrast, one liberal Catholic magazine I saw this week featured as a cover story "What Will You Take Up for Lent?" The idea, of course, is that giving things up has too negative a connotation and is too individualistic; what we need to do, the magazine suggests, is instead to take up a positive practice this Lent, one that will help the poor.

In today's first reading, Isaiah (58:9b–14) gives the lie to the false dichotomy between individual piety and concern for the collective welfare of all. Isaiah lambasts the Israelites *both* for neglecting the religious practices crucial for personal holiness *and* for oppressing the poor. Particularly, he implores the people to repent by honoring the Sabbath (13) and ceasing to oppress and starve the poor (10). God's promise to restore the land holds only if both problems are addressed (14).

Isaiah—and the Church that asks us to contemplate Isaiah at the beginning of Lent—is wiser and possesses a better understanding of human psychology than do modern conservatives or liberals. The practices of personal holiness are means of learning self-control and of processing that we are in fact not our own; we have no right of ownership over our time, our food, our money, or anything we possess. Practically speaking, if we haven't learned to honor the Sabbath and to tithe (to give God our time and our money), what are the odds that we'll ever give others our time or share our money? If we haven't learned that what we have isn't our own, what are the odds that we'll share it? The traditional understanding of Lent as a time both of personal asceticism and of aid for the poor has it exactly right—these disciplines are linked.

I've had countless opportunities to observe this truth over the course of my life. Public college English departments are one of the few remaining places in the United States that you will find anyone who self-identifies as a Marxist. I shared an office in graduate school with a fellow who flew the Soviet flag over his desk long after the fall of the Soviet Union, and I presently work with at least two professors who call themselves Marxists. They are careful scholars and dedicated teachers; they are paradoxes only when evaluated as Marxists, as revolutionary advocates for social justice. Their houses are twice the size of mine and they are more likely to go on about (respectively) their sports car or Viking cooking range than to lay down their lives for the proletariat. Professors of this sort are generous in theory, but not in practice; lacking any ascetic training, they simply do the things they enjoy (like reading books about social class and drinking craft beer) and neglect the things they don't (like working in a food pantry or serving at a soup kitchen or donating money).

By the same token, I've known many Evangelical Protestants (such as my father) who were not generous in theory—they would blame the poor for their own plight, reciting Paul's dictum "He who does not work, neither shall he eat"—but who were generous in practice (I grew up with a succession of homeless people living in the basement). They had learned the disciplines that make care for others possible and so *did* care for others, whether they theoretically believed in taking care of others or not. (I don't know how much of this rubbed off on me. All I remember about sharing the house with a homeless teen is that he always beat me at Monopoly.)

I have given up watching television this Lent, hoping thereby to cause my perceptions of the world to be shaped more by the liturgical calendar than by the prime-time lineup; I have acted traditionally. And, as a result, I am encountering Isaiah, who begins to make me wonder whether I should join my parish's Social Justice Committee and whether I should be giving more to the poor.

Monday of the First Week in Lent
(Lev 19:1–2, 11–18)

Today I don't feel particularly interested in justice, self-sacrifice, or helping others. What has driven Lent out of my head? The next-door neighbor, a tattooed twentysomething teacher at a private elementary school, has now dumped a third dead automobile into her backyard. I'm sure—rightly, as it turns out—that before the day is out my wife and I will be discussing whether the neighborhood is going downhill and whether we should move. We're as deep and as spiritual as the average appliance salesman.

Today's reading from Leviticus (19:1–2, 11–18) commands, "Love your neighbor as yourself" (18), and I might begin by taking this point literally. My father left my mother when I was a teen; a period of financial difficulty and struggle followed for my mother, sister, and me (my brother had long been out of the house). I'm well aware that in 1991 my family had two dead cars in the backyard; we were the house with teenage kids blaring punk music; we were the house in disrepair (cracked driveway, busted central air-conditioning unit, collapsing porch, bad siding, peeling wallpaper, broken particleboard cabinets, carpet that reeked of dog urine).[1]

I remember why the house was in disrepair; it wasn't negligence. We had purchased the house as a fixer-upper, and six months later my father left the family—and with him went both the skills and the money needed to fix the house. The fixer-upper was never fixed.

I remember why the dead cars—an AMC Alliance and an AMC Eagle, cars produced by a manufacturer that had even then ceased to exist—were in our backyard. It wasn't an exercise in aesthetics or an attempt to spite our neighbors. We were too broke to fix them, and too broke to replace them. So the cars had to sit there, sometimes for many months, as we scraped the funds together to

---

[1] My mother, who is fond of her house, would want you to know that she has made improvements.

bring at least one of them back to life; in the meantime, we worked out precarious carpooling schedules to get to work and school.

As we puttered down the street in whichever car was for the moment barely working, my sister and I would point and shout, "There goes the neighborhood!" We were pointing at our own house. My neighbor as myself, indeed.

I don't know whether my wife and I should stay at our current location or move. I can hardly give meaningful input into the discussion. I don't tend to notice my surroundings and have actually driven up to the neighbor's home thinking it was my own (notwithstanding the fact that hers is brick, while ours is aluminum sided).[2] Anything stylish, aesthetically pleasing, or even functionally useful in our house can be traced directly back to my wife.

But I do know that it must be a good thing that I haven't moved someplace where I will never meet anyone who struggles to make ends meet. We've never done anything to help our next-door neighbor, whom I know struggles to pay a mass of college debt with a paycheck barely larger than a cashier's, and have rarely even spoken to her. She just sits chain-smoking on her cluttered porch, where the trim is torn off and wood has begun to rot; she has few visitors. Loving your neighbor perhaps begins with knowing your neighbor. Jesus' teaching surpasses the Old Law. But apparently I haven't made it to Leviticus yet.

Friday of the First Week in Lent (Ezek 18:21–28)

The religious tradition in which I was raised heavily emphasized the wrath of God. When the other local

---

[2] Here Emily corrected the manuscript, crossing out "aluminum sided" and writing "vinyl sided". We had lived in our house for almost seven years when I wrote that sentence. I told you that I did not notice my surroundings.

churches decided to put on a play, they did something heartwarming about the true meaning of Christmas. We, on the other hand, put on a play called *Heaven's Gates, Hell's Flames*. The title says it all. As the devil (stage right) narrates his designs to the audience, unsuspecting sinners playing golf or drinking beer (center stage) are suddenly caught up and thrown by demons through a trapdoor into hell (stage left), where—as a creepy, distorted voice booms over the loudspeakers—"there will be weeeeping and gnashing of teeeeeeth."

So some part of me is still surprised—and deeply impressed—by the calm rationality of today's reading from Ezekiel (18:21–28). Ezekiel suggests that God has no particular desire to punish anyone; he "derive[s] no pleasure from the death of the wicked" (23). God created the universe and made its laws. Therefore, if you act in holiness, you act in accord with the basic principles on which the universe was designed, and you should generally reap good results. If you act in defiance of the divine, you act against the basic principles on which the universe was designed, and you will generally reap bad results. It's as logical and impersonal as math, and Ezekiel reminds us that these options stand always before us. Whether we think of ourselves as just or wicked doesn't much matter. We are continually faced with the option of conforming ourselves to the universe or imagining that it will simply conform to us. The same action (just or unjust) will produce the same result (good or bad), regardless of who performs it (cf. 24, 27). God can certainly claim that his ways are "fair" (25). The wrath of God is simply our subjective experience of our approach to the universe not working out.

My daughter, not yet two years old, often complains that chairs, tables, and walls attack her and are mean to her. "The chair hu-u-urted me," she will moan. And I don't doubt that it did hurt when she ran barefoot into our sizable black wooden living-room chair. But the chair has a particular wrath against her only from her own very subjective position.

Lent is a period in which we attempt to adjust ourselves to God's universe and accept his terms. The Collect prays that we may "be so conformed to the paschal observances, that the bodily discipline now solemnly begun may bear fruit in the souls of all". By conforming ourselves exteriorly (through bodily discipline) to the pattern of the world revealed in the Eucharist (Christ's self-renunciation and entrance into glory), we begin to be interiorly conformed to the principles on which God's world operates, and our souls begin to flower.

Thursday of the Second Week in Lent (Lk 16:19–31)

Today we read the story of the rich man and Lazarus (Lk 16:19–31). In the afterlife, a poor man and a rich man find their roles reversed: the beggar Lazarus is embraced by Abraham and received by God into the glories of heaven, while the uncharitable rich man suffers eternal torments from which he unsuccessfully begs to be relieved. A fitting story for Lent.

When I read this Gospel, I'm taken back in memory to my summer 1991 visit to Chicago with my oldest friend (we've known each other since third grade). He is a tall blond aesthete who has turned an art history degree into a career in independent book sales. Whenever I go anywhere with him, I'm his sidekick as he plots our routes and often leads me through places I would never consider going on my own. He is perpetually restless and curious and more or less devoid of fear. This time, we stayed (quite deliberately) on the north side of Chicago at a dive motel where the hallways smelled like vomit. Various alternative rock bands that he enjoys had lodged there while on tour early in their careers and later complained about the experience; he had to smell the vomit for himself. Then we drifted about the city on the elevated train, stopping whenever he glimpsed a piece of architecture that interested him and wandering at length through the adjacent neighborhoods. We were often ludicrously—perhaps imprudently—out of place, two obviously vulnerable and naïve college students. Disoriented after a day spent everywhere, we found our way back to our hotel late at night only by bribing a homeless guy to give us directions.

One Chicago scene for which Detroit life hadn't prepared me was starkly juxtaposed opulence and squalor. Million-dollar luxury condominiums stood a block from tenements, both blocking the sky. The Detroit area is full of both luxury and squalor, but since Detroit is one of the largest cities in North America in terms of landmass, they're separated by a seemingly infinite gradual ascent or descent. The very rich virtually never live next to the very poor. They live next to the rich, who live next to the pretty rich, who live next to the upper-middle class, and so on and so forth. In Detroit, the rich man would probably never get the opportunity to meet Lazarus, and I sometimes think that in essence this is the goal of modern urban planning.

I stood with my aesthete friend, hot and sunburned on a day in early July, taking in the condominiums and the tenements, straining to see the sky. A thinly bearded African American man in his midforties walked up to us, took a hit off a fifth of whiskey, and then asked for money. My friend characteristically gave him a five and asked him to tell us about the city. Instead, the man looked conspiratorially at us and whispered, "Do you know your Bibles? Do

you have the truth? You're never gonna know the truth
if you don't know the Bible. People lie, but the Bible will
tell you the way things really are."

I assured him that we did know our Bibles, and he pro-
ceeded to recount the story of the rich man and Lazarus
at great length and with increasing volume, concluding,
"That's how it is. God hasn't quit watching." He shook
his fist at the condominiums. "We're going to party and
they're going to pay." It was a surreal moment. I felt
like I had stepped into a Flannery O'Connor novel. Then
he shouted at a female yuppie passerby, "Will you love
me, baby?" and drifted off in her direction too slowly and
aimlessly to catch her nervous and hurried steps.

But, while the drunken sidewalk prophet's exegesis
wasn't nuanced, neither was it totally unsound. Jesus often
depicts the future as a reversal of the present, envisioning
a future in which the rich are abased and the poor are
exalted. This parable should disturb us. To embrace the
Gospel is to challenge the established order and to question the way things are—and the way we are. It's also to be
unsettled, to place ourselves consciously before the divine
judgment and await the outcome, here (we hope) rather
than hereafter. And that's what Lent is all about.

Annunciation of the Lord (March 26)[3] (Lk 1:26–38)

Today's Gospel—Luke 1:26–38, the Annunciation story—
shows us that the Word precedes the Incarnation, the
spiritual idea comes before the material person or thing.
The angel's annunciation precedes Mary's conception of

---

[3] The Annunciation is normally celebrated on March 25, but it was moved
to March 26 in this year because March 25 was the Fifth Sunday of Lent.

Jesus. This is the pattern going back to the divine word that brings about creation; "the universe was ordered by the word of God" (Heb 11:3, NABRE[4]). God speaks (in this case through his angelic messenger), and things come into being.

At its heart, faith is not an ad hoc explanation of things that already exist, a way of trying to impose meaning and pattern on an arbitrary universe; faith is why anything at all is there to explain. Hebrews tells us that faith is the "substance of things hoped for, the evidence of things unseen" (11:1, KJV[5]). It is the *evidence* of things unseen because the word of faith participates in the eternal Word that creates and sustains the universe. Hebrews 11 speaks of the creation story and the Abraham narrative as examples of faith because in each case the divine word speaks the event into being before it exists in any material form that we can see. For the nation of Israel (and by extension the Church) as for the universe itself, "What is visible came into being through the invisible" (Heb 11:3, NABRE). To have faith, then, is not to believe against all material evidence (as many skeptics and some Christians have thought); to have faith is to accord with the basic structure of reality. Unless the world itself is utterly devoid of meaning and human cognition is a joke, the word, the idea, must always precede the thing. Faith precedes material existence. C.S. Lewis knew this, and Plato knew this, but no one puts it better than the author of Hebrews.

And what more perfect example of this definition of faith than Mary in her fiat: "Let it be done unto me according to thy word" (Lk 1:38)? The moment she embraces the divine word, the Word takes on flesh. The Feast of the

[4] NABRE = New American Bible, Revised Edition.
[5] KJV = King James Version.

Annunciation gets at the heart of why faith is necessary at all and what it means to have faith. It's easy for me to wax high rhetorical and to have grand thoughts about it; it's central to my faith and to how I understand reality.

But here's a less exalted story: over the last two days, my wife and I have begun awkwardly, hesitantly discussing in a manner hedged about with qualifications whether we should have a second child. These discussions have taken place in bed, late at night, after our daughter has gone to sleep. They consist mostly of mumbling and stuttering, but the gist is clear.

"Hmmm . . . ," Emily says. She is lying on her back, and I can't see her face. But I know from her intonation—starting low and deep and ending even lower and deeper—exactly what she means: we really need to think about child rearing. We're getting older. The biological clock is ticking. The time is right.

"Well . . . ," I reply, pronouncing the word as "whale" and stretching it into three syllables, as I typically do when nervous and stuck for something to say. Then I trail off. And Emily knows exactly what I mean: every fifteen minutes of our schedule is managed every day as it is. The whole system barely works. Our lives as we know them will collapse if we add one or more children to the mix.

Then I turn toward the window and she turns toward the wall. And we try to sleep.

An hour later, we're both back on our backs looking up at the ceiling. I say, "Hmmm," which Emily knows means that I see—and might be getting ready to cede—her point.

She replies, "Well," which I know means she has come around to mine. We've switched sides. This "conversation" continues for half the night. We've resolved nothing, but the door to another child is now just barely cracked open.

I know that openness to a second child doesn't constitute heroic virtue. It may even fall short of ordinary virtue.

But as I've admitted, Emily and I are all too aware of the conveniences and attractions of barrenness; they have been embraced by just about everyone who attended graduate school with us. And we don't exist entirely apart from the environment that surrounds us.

It was a faith decision for us to have one child in the first place. It's been a graced experience that we in no way regret—but also one we're just learning how to handle. A first child meant a certain loss of control, a certain challenge to our egoism. But with careful planning, our lives could still continue on the same trajectory as before; the ship rocks but remains upright. A multichild family means a different life, one whose course we truly cannot set ourselves. And we like to be in control.

But Lent is precisely about challenging and questioning the lives we daily lead and the values we typically assume. And the Annunciation is all about being open to the divine word. The divine command is "Be fruitful and multiply" (Gen 9:1, RSV2CE[6]); God doesn't seem to care whether we *feel* fruitful or particularly wish to multiply. Emily and I do trust God more than we trust ourselves, and we undertook this Lent in all sincerity. So we say on this Feast of the Annunciation, "Let it be done to us according to your word—maybe? If it's *really* necessary? If you're sure?"

Palm Sunday of the Passion of the Lord
(Mk 14:1–15:47)

Palm Sunday Mass is a very different experience when viewed from the perspective of a not-quite-two-year-old. We arrived at church today at the last second and had to sit in the pews way up at the front and to the side. They're

[6] RSV2CE = Revised Standard Version, 2nd Catholic Edition.

usually the last ones left, since they give a sideways view of the altar and place the worshipper at a right angle to the rest of the congregation. But Beatrice loved the view; from up there, she could see everybody and everything. I don't know how well she followed the finer points of the liturgy, but she liked waving a palm, and she liked that everyone else was waving a palm too. She loves to shout out during Mass (at both appropriate and inappropriate moments), and she was delighted that this time everyone joined her: we all shouted out at various parts of the Gospel reading (Mk 14:1–15:47), if only to say, "Crucify him!" She looked around and smiled her crooked smile in gleeful disbelief. "This is a church," my daughter clearly thought today, "to which I can really belong; everyone is just like me."

The earthy materiality of the Catholic Church has no natural appeal to me (I prefer abstract intellectual systems), but it shows the Church's wisdom. At twenty-three months, Beatrice already recognizes images of Jesus, Mary, and Joseph and knows they are central figures in her life. Despite our injunctions to be quiet, she shouts greetings to the statue of Mary each time we enter the nave. She can participate in worship through material objects like the palm in ways that get into the warp and woof of consciousness before she can fully understand in any explicit sense what she is doing. In the divine mind, the thought or word precedes the thing, but for us, the material thing is primary and the thought comes, well, as an afterthought. Beatrice may have been right to think that we are all mentally on the same page.

She may also have understood what she was doing about as well as the mob did on the original Palm Sunday. It's fun to lay down palms and to hail a new king. It's fun to have hope for deliverance. It's also fun to shout for crucifixion, to jeer someone unpopular, of whom one can safely disapprove. What's difficult is transforming the whole way one views kingship and power, imagining what it means to worship a king who rules the world from a Cross. What's difficult is realizing that Jesus is destroying the way the world has always run and calling into question everything it seemed we could safely assume. What can you count on, the saying runs, except death and taxes (which is to say, the futility of human existence and the self-serving nature of power)? And now Jesus is showing us that we can't count on them either. It's no wonder we have trouble understanding and embracing this new world he is showing us.

Where Beatrice is different from the original Palm Sunday mob is that she eventually tried to eat the palm, and I had to wrestle it away from her.

Good Friday of the Passion of the Lord

I don't understand why it's so hard to find a Virginia Catholic church that offers some sort of service at noon on Good Friday. It's always been a practice of mine, since I first began frequenting Catholic churches long before my conversion, to honor noon to three o'clock on Good Friday, the hours when Jesus was undergoing his Passion. In the Detroit area, where I am from, plenty of parishes run devotional observances continually for all three hours. I know that people have to work and have difficulty getting time off, but the absence of these traditional devotions does bother me. These are the hours when the world stopped, when life became devoid of meaning, when Nietzsche was right and God was dead, the pillar and support on which being rests was suspended, and teleology and existence itself became questionable or nullified. These are hours that *should* halt and interrupt our lives. There is something appalling about failing to observe these three hours to accommodate our schedule. Jesus was killed because we found him difficult to accommodate. This suggests who our gods truly are. The workday rules, and Christ is a hobby.

All I've been able to manage in central Virginia is an ecumenical service held at noon in the town where I work (occasionally the Catholic priest participates, most often not). Since the Solemn Intercessions of the Good Friday liturgy include a long prayer for the unity of Christians, at least I can have the consolation of knowing that my presence at this service accords with the thoughts of the liturgy for today. If there is one place where Christ's dispersed followers should be able to gather together, it should be at the foot of the Cross; if there was one prayer Jesus prayed in his Passion, it was for the unity of the flock.

In a mostly empty church, an aging crowd, with a sprinkling of college students, suspend the activities of their day to acknowledge the crucified Lord. Though I always enjoy the pipe organ (played quite excellently by an extremely quiet and very thin French professor at our college), the service itself isn't usually particularly memorable. But the final moment redeems all. The service always concludes with the book of the Gospel being slammed dramatically shut—a kind of Protestant equivalent of the Maundy Thursday stripping of the altar—and the congregation departing in silence; the eternal Word is now silent. For the rest of today and tomorrow, we will endure the silence of God and live in this emptiness.

4

A HOLY CHAOS?
(Easter Time)

Easter Sunday of the Resurrection of the Lord (Easter Vigil Mass) (Gen 1:1–2:2; Ezek 36:16–17a, 18–28)

Easter Vigil Mass. We all gather on a Southern spring night around a dignified brick fire pit. Until this year—really, until an Eagle Scout intervened and built the fire pit—on this holiest of nights we lit the paschal candle that symbolizes the light of Christ off a sputtering backyard bonfire or an underpowered barbecue grill. Our new roaring fire, which shoots flames several feet into the air and seems a light that really could conquer the night, better reflects God's transcendent, burning love.

But the Church embraces both the sacred and the profane. While I waited for the service to start, I saw that I was standing near an acquaintance who had recently been laid off from his job working for an electrical contractor. (While his wife works, he takes his children to the same coffee shop that I frequent, so our orbits have inevitably crossed.) Tonight his eight-year-old daughter gave me the good news: "Daddy has a new job with the city. He fixes the machines that count the poop." Then she ran off to get us all the candles that would carry the light of Christ.

The Easter Vigil is the most boring and the most moving of Masses. Seven separate Old Testament readings narrate the story of salvation history. They take us all the way from humanity's mundane origins in the dirt and the mire (Gen 1:1–2:2) to its exalted destiny: the possession of a "new heart" and a "new spirit" bestowed directly by God (Ezek 36:26, from the seventh reading, Ezek 36:16–17a, 18–28). As you listen, and listen, and listen, you experience the Jewish people's long wait for redemption. If you're sleepy, you begin to wonder, as the Jews did, when will the Messiah ever come? When will the lights be lit? How long can we remain awake and alert?

In the homily, the deacon said that in the early Church the verbal exchange "He is risen"—"He is risen indeed" functioned as a kind of pass code for entrance into Christian ritual. To know these words, to enter this exchange, was also to enter the Eucharistic community. This is still the case now, almost two thousand years later. Even now, we enter the church on the Easter Vigil seeking only—for what else is there to seek?—Christ's resurrected life.

Tuesday within the Octave of Easter (Jn 20:11–18)

Today's Gospel (Jn 20:11–18) is certainly one of the more powerful Resurrection accounts. Mary Magdalene sees Jesus but conceptually cannot understand what she is seeing and mistakes him for the gardener. Jesus is often almost unrecognizable in the Resurrection stories. In part, Jesus cannot be recognized because of who he is. He is not simply resuscitated from death; he is risen into a new mode of existence in which matter participates but in which the normal limitations that we associate with matter do not apply. He has a body (he eats fish, for example), but it is not like our body (*I* don't walk through walls or suddenly materialize in a room).

In part, Jesus cannot be recognized because of weaknesses in the perceiver. We see based upon our frame of reference, and we process most easily information that fits into that frame. Since it *can't* be Jesus that Mary is seeing—he is dead—she can't possibly see the person she has encountered as Jesus, even when he is literally staring her in the face. Maybe this is why Jesus warns Mary, "Stop holding on to me, for I have not yet ascended to the Father" (17). To hold on to Jesus is to render him finite, to crystallize him within our frame of reference rather than to allow him to raise us up to his. I wonder how many times Jesus has had to tell me to quit holding on to him and instead to look up to the heavens, where he sits at the right hand of the Father. I wonder how many times he will have to say it this year.

Monday of the Second Week of Easter (Jn 3:1–8)

The Gospel reading for today (Jn 3:1–8) is the story of the Pharisee Nicodemus questioning Jesus privately, in secret, at night. Nicodemus' botched attempts to understand the Gospel make for a scene ripe with metaphysical comedy. Jesus explains that a person "cannot see the Kingdom of God" unless he experiences a second birth and is "born from above". Nicodemus incredulously replies, "How can a man once grown old be born again? Surely he cannot re-enter his mother's womb and be born again, can he?" (3, 4). Here Jesus is talking about spiritual rebirth, and Nicodemus replies by worrying about whether he could still physically fit inside his mother. Jesus is speaking in a symbolic register, and Nicodemus is thinking solely in terms of the literal. Scholars call this "Johannine irony". The less educated might call it "cross talk". Nicodemus functions as a surrogate for the literal-minded reader, as the text tries to train us in how to read God's world and understand God.

But Nicodemus' objections perhaps shouldn't be so easily brushed aside. Being spiritually reborn hurts. Birth is scary. Children (and their mothers) scream. No one wants to go through it. And who, having done it once, would want to do it again? Part of the trouble with birth is that you're leaving a world where you understood the rules and entering one in which everything that you've previously known no longer applies. You no longer get your food through an umbilical cord. You're no longer kept warm in the uterus but are exposed to the elements. And so on. Entering a new world in which eternal life is possible—but in which you can no longer simply please yourself and seek your own aims—is at least as confusing as being born. It's awkward, it's difficult, and it's painful.

My sister spent her teenage years in a self-destructive spiral, from which she has since escaped by the grace of God. She remains eager to help other edgy and troubled souls, whether by teaching English skills to at-risk inner-city students or by bringing faith to depressed nihilists. Back in the 1990s, she took a bartender friend of hers—a person spiritually curious but uncommitted, a "seeker", as they say—to a multiday Christian music festival. At the Cornerstone Festival everyone would camp out on a vast mud plane near the Mississippi River, attending rock concerts and theological lectures and neglecting sanitation. Between events, my sister's short, redheaded, paper-thin friend kept seeing "hot" guys pass her tent and tried to pick them up as she would have at a bar: batted her eyelashes, tossed her hair, giggled fake laughter, showed a glimpse of skin. She was baffled when the men looked at each other in confusion, shrugged, then hurried away to the next event. She didn't get this new world where the tried-and-true strategies of the strictly material universe in which she lived and moved—the meat-market singles bar—no longer applied.

I'm no better, really. I'll catch myself in the confessional booth rhetorically framing my sins—admitting the action but using every English-major trick I've got to cast the motive in as glorious terms as I can. We try to approach Christ's new life with the old strategies, and they just don't work. We can't live in the old way anymore—we can't just go back into the womb—and we don't yet know how to live in the new. To his credit, Nicodemus at least realizes how different the world Jesus offers actually is.

Fourth Sunday of Easter (1 Jn 3:1–2)

Today I took Beatrice to the student Mass at Lynchburg College. Put a portable altar on wheels in a colonial-style Protestant chapel, and you get the perfect setting for Virginia Catholicism. The Mass is delivered where the Catholic writer (and friend of C. S. Lewis) Sheldon Vanauken once gave lay sermons. The people are friendly, and the priest is dignified. I really like going to Mass here. There is just one problem: the place is dead silent, and there is neither a cry room nor a real narthex. Beatrice made it, as usual, about halfway through the service before she began shouting and had to be carried out. Between the homily and the Our Father, she walked around on the campus green, jumped on and off of stone benches, climbed into and out of brightly colored wooden chairs, ate dried cranberries, read her *Pride and Prejudice* board book, and all in all regained her equilibrium. Then we dashed back in, and she received a blessing as I received the Eucharist. As we left, she told me she liked the music. I'll never know exactly what she takes away from these Masses or what she is thinking.

The epistle today (1 Jn 3:1–2) asserts that we are part of God's Kingdom now, though we can't imagine the nature and shape this Kingdom will finally take. We can only partly imagine even our own redeemed selves since they will be the reflection of the resurrected Christ, whom we cannot at all imagine. "What we shall be has not yet been revealed" (2). Life is full of continuity and disjunction, and as the Anglican poet Christina Rossetti realized, we see the true picture and glimpse the actual pattern only retrospectively, from heaven.[1]

To offer an analogy: at the age of thirteen, I vowed I would spend my life as a homeless poet living in the beauties of the Blue Ridge Mountains. Yes, I was that pompous and that impractical. Also, I had only ever been on one vacation. The Blue Ridge was my only concrete mental image of a world outside of metro Detroit. There is something tremendously thirteen about this vow's combination of absolute determination and utter absurdity. But there are through lines between my past and present self, albeit not ones I could have imagined at that time. I am not homeless and I am not a poet, just a rather conventional family man with a job. But I do study and teach poetry in the foothills of the Blue Ridge Mountains. The dreams of my youth are at once farcically stupid and strangely prophetic. I trust that my present life will also be both appropriate and ridiculous when viewed in light of my life in eternity.

Perhaps this is true for Beatrice as well, who loves at Mass to shake hands and say "Peace" but who, not yet

---

[1] See Rossetti's poem "Looking Back", from her collection *Verses* (London: SPCK, 1893).

knowing conflict, cannot conceptualize what peace is, much less the peace of Christ. Yet, she intuitively grasps that there is something wonderful in this exchange; she is already living in a world she cannot yet comprehend. As are we. We are always living lives that make only retrospective sense; given what happens later, the present is always a comedy. All baptisms are infant baptisms.

Fifth Sunday of Easter (Acts 9:26–31; Jn 15:1–8)

As my daughter was getting dressed this morning, she predicted the course of her Sunday morning (accurately, as it turns out): "I will see Father. Go to Catholic church. I will say 'Hi' to him. I will shake hands with him. I will show him my Mingo." She stomped into the church and offered a hand to the priest, who gravely shook it, very formally greeted her, and bravely tried not to recoil at the sight of her now-graying stuffed flamingo.

This week, we had a children's Liturgy of the Word. The children were dismissed after the Gloria, to return at the Liturgy of the Eucharist. They tramped into a small side chapel where they all sat on the floor in a semicircle around their catechist and an early-model CD player (what once would have been called a "boom box").

Today's first reading (Acts 9:26–31) relates Saul's arrival in Jerusalem and the initially skeptical reception the Church gives him until the trustworthy and optimistic Barnabas intervenes with the apostles on his behalf. The catechist began the lesson by asking the children about their friends. Then, hyperextending her neck and jutting out her lips like a duck, she told the kids that Saul was a "grumpy" person who didn't like Jesus and who didn't want anyone else to be friends with Jesus. Then Saul met

Jesus and was accepted, after some uncertainty, by Jesus' friends. The moral of her story: Friends all around. Then "Jesus Loves Me" blasted from the boom box, we all sang along loudly and dissonantly, and we tramped back into the nave just in time for the Prayers of the Faithful.

My own cast of mind is theological and intellectual. I would rather talk about the *homoousion* than shake anyone's hand.[2] So, during the lesson, whatever part of my mind wasn't occupied with constraining my daughter from running around the room was horrified at the catechist's rendering of Scripture. The astute Pharisee Saul was just a grumpy guy who needed a resurrected friend? "Horrors", as Lowly Worm is wont to say in many a Richard Scarry book.

But at dinner, I asked two-year-old Beatrice what the stories in Mass were about, and she quickly replied, "Saul—he were grumpy." Which was a better result than I would have obtained. Today's Gospel (Jn 15:1–8) is the parable of the vine and the branches, relating how each Christian grows as an offshoot of Christ and derives life only from him. Perhaps I shouldn't overtheorize the process by which a new twig springs from the vine.

Saturday of the Fifth Week of Easter

Today's Collect is beautiful:

> Almighty and eternal God,
> who through the regenerating power of Baptism
> have been pleased to confer on us heavenly life,

---

[2] The term *homoousion* refers to the idea that Jesus is of one substance with the Father.

grant, we pray,
that those you render capable of immortality
by justifying them
may by your guidance
attain the fullness of glory.

By coincidence or Providence, the Church has offered a perfect prayer for this graduation Saturday. God has through baptism, which encapsulates and enacts our death and resurrection with Christ, given us a capacity for the transcendent and eternal beyond that which we naturally possess. We have been rendered "capable of immortality" (what a fine phrase!). We have been given, as a gift and through no real merit of our own, the ability to transcend ourselves and our natural state. Our lives and identities need not be the warped products of a brutal Darwinian struggle for survival. But, after we have been baptized, we still have to learn to live in this "heavenly life". Our lives after baptism present us with an ever-changing myriad of complicated situations, in all of which we can live the "heavenly life" if we continually seek the "guidance" of God. If we remain faithful, when we die our enduring pursuit of the divine life will receive its logical (and graciously excessive) reward: we will ultimately "attain the fullness of glory". If, on the other hand, we don't after baptism strive to live the heavenly life, then our capacity for immortality remains a mere potentiality, never actualized, a tragedy rather than a joy.

In a sense, college graduation, in which I served a role today as a faculty member, can serve as an analogy. Though the student does have to work hard to get the degree (unlike baptism, it is not simply a gift conferred—or at least one hopes it is not simply a gift conferred), what the degree gives the student is the capacity both to have a career in a particular chosen field and to think at a generally higher level. But this capacity has to be inhabited and actuated; there is necessarily a gap between receiving the abstract knowledge that gives the potential for greater things and concretely actuating that knowledge. Free will and circumstance come into play. College can bestow the capacity; it can't bestow the life.

Alumni often come back to the college to visit, particularly on graduation day, when the campus green is festively decorated, "Pomp and Circumstance" is blaring, and hope and nostalgia fill the air. Some of these students will have fallen into despair and will have resigned themselves to lifelong restaurant work (a fate that was nearly my own; I graduated in the middle of a recession, and I initially commemorated my degree only by taking on extra hours running the drive-through window). One of the brightest students I have ever taught—an extremely tall and extremely shy science major with an English minor—remains a barista to this day. One former student got an entry-level job working in radio upon graduation—the culmination of a successful internship—then decided he would rather spend his life moving boxes at a Walmart warehouse. Some will have gotten professional jobs—sometimes, alarmingly, as English teachers—but won't have read a book since graduation. Others will be both contributing to society and continuing to develop intellectually; many of my former students have become better high school teachers than I ever had.

I'm often wrong when I try to predict a student's future. I imagined that the biologist would make both brilliant discoveries and a brilliant career and that the DJ would keep spinning tunes. When I foresee a negative outcome, I'm just as frequently mistaken. A sorority girl I busted for plagiarism now wins teaching awards, and a slacker of an

English major who always got a merciful C from me is now rising high—and doing much good—in the federal government. No student's end result can really be foreseen. For, like the life of grace, the life of the mind too requires actuation.

From my perch behind the stage, I watched over a thousand people receive their degrees today, but one was undoubtedly the highlight for me: our best English major, graduating magna cum laude. She came running over to greet me after the ceremony. Apart from the graduation robe, she has wrapped herself physically and metaphysically in bohemian chic—short hair, chunky plastic retro glasses, peasant dress, social-justice Anglicanism. I assumed that she was chasing me down to introduce me to her family, which was true. But it turned out that, more important, she was having trouble working through a certain aspect of the thought of the German philosopher Martin Heidegger. She was determined to corral enough professors for an impromptu panel on the subject before she was willing to walk off the campus green and into her future. She is a hyperactive intellectual idealist and, flamboyance aside, basically a near-perfect embodiment of the liberal arts education our public college hopes to offer. She seems the perfect—and inevitable—product of the ivory tower.

But everything looks inevitable when you start your story at the end and leave out the middle. She is twenty-eight. Between freshman year (also spent at our college) and graduation, she underwent a troubled marriage, multiple college transfers, a season as a college dropout, a divorce (not her fault), a crisis of faith, and a restoration of faith and well-being. Whatever reservations I might have about her theology, the persistence of her faith is a miracle. And her presence here today is a work of grace.

Other good moments of the day included seeing a graduate from several years back who suffered a psychological breakdown her senior year, now come back to her old school to watch her friends graduate; to my delight, she is now emotionally stable and gainfully employed in the field of education, still in church, and talking about G. K. Chesterton.

In *The Last Battle*, C. S. Lewis compared the end of the school term to the end of time, when we leave finitude behind and enter into the rest of God. One hopes that from heaven one will likewise look back from baptism to resurrection and see how God's guidance has led us into the fullness of glory.

Tuesday of the Sixth Week in Easter (Acts 16:29–32)

Today my wife and I are back to talking about moving, about houses we might purchase and neighborhoods in which we might desire to live. Or, rather, my wife is, and I'm trying to keep my replies to a polite nod and a weak smile. Sometimes I'm more successful than others:

EMILY: I keep going on about everything I want in a house. But I don't want this house thing to be all about what I want. I'm not comfortable with that. There must be something you want.

CHENE: I'd like a very elaborate headstone. You know: large, limestone, lots of ornate carvings, maybe some poetry etched on something that looks like a scroll.

But even this response elicits merely an awkward pause. Then the weighing of the positives and negatives of particular houses and neighborhoods resumes.

The only thing concerning this discussion about which I am certain is that there is good reason to distrust both of us. We each have good motives and bad motives for our respective positions, and these motives are hopelessly mixed together. For instance, Emily really enjoys architecture, decorating, and cooking for large groups of people. She is an Aristotelian and possesses a more vibrant appreciation of materiality and the created world than I do. She is also more of a do-it-yourselfer and always loves a project (and our small house is running out of potential projects; it has been project-ed to death). However, she is also more prone to external pressure than I am, and her professor and administrator friends are busy buying big houses. She may be unconsciously just trying to keep up.

I am a Platonist, indifferent to my material surroundings—so long as I have a good book—and I care little for the opinions of others. I also grew up in worse neighborhoods and smaller houses than my wife did; to me, our house doesn't seem small. Positively, I disdain materialism and elitism. Negatively, my refusal to be attached to material things is due as much to Henry David Thoreau's "quiet desperation" as to holy asceticism. Sigmund Freud observed that when we refuse object attachments, we are generally withdrawing into ourselves for purposes of self-protection, and I can recognize myself in the diagnosis. My teenage years—dominated by my parents' divorce, my sister's years'-long dalliance with drug culture, and our broken family's downward economic mobility—have left me with the sense that nothing in this world can be counted on over the long haul and that existence is best faced with a detached bemusement. I know that this attitude sounds more like Buddha than Jesus, but still—I'm never going to get excited about a house, any house.

In short, no one is obviously morally right here. We both have the defects of our virtues and the virtues of our defects. We have no idea how to resolve this, so the discussion just continues. Emily seems for the moment set on a stucco Victorian in the old-money part of town, which was built back during the Reconstruction by carpetbaggers like ourselves.

EMILY: Of course, if we buy this house, I'll want to make some changes.

CHENE: I've come to accept that whatever house we own, you will gradually replace every single piece of it over time, just as each cell in the human body is replaced every seven years.

This gets an eye roll, but then the seemingly unstoppable discussion resumes.

So how on earth do we resolve this? As yet, we have no idea. One thing I really don't understand in marriage is how to manage disagreement productively. How do you support your spouse without simply being an appendage? I know that it bothers my wife that I don't echo back her feelings about house and neighborhood. This makes her feel like she is on her own on this one—as, in truth, she is—and that makes her feel like a bad person. And then she understandably reacts against this.

But if you just become an echo chamber, how does iron sharpen iron? And certainly, she has never been an echo chamber for me (nor would I want one). Her parents invariably seem to agree, mine to disagree. If you always agree, how do you strengthen and complement each other? If you always disagree, how do you have any unity at all? So how do two people become one flesh? How do you actually make a unit that is more than one person writ large?

In today's reading from the book of Acts (16:29–32), Paul and Silas are thrown in jail for preaching the Gospel and are miraculously freed by means of an earthquake but remain in prison out of compassion for the jailer, who would be executed if his prisoners escaped. The stunned jailer then accepts the Gospel, and Paul promises salvation both to him and his family: "Believe in the Lord Jesus and you and your household will be saved" (31). In many ways, this is what I'm asking—how can we experience salvation as a family? How can the family unit truly be a salvific structure? Paul promises; it must be possible. But I don't have a clear answer yet.

Thursday of the Sixth Week of Easter (Jn 16:16–20)

In my diocese, today is Thursday of the Sixth Week of Easter. But in the rest of the Catholic world, today is Ascension Thursday (to keep holy days of obligation to a minimum, we lazily move the feast to the following Sunday). So today I am reflecting on the readings for an ordinary Thursday but am thinking about the Ascension.

I never really understood anything about the Ascension until I had to read the Anglo-Saxon poet Cynewulf in graduate school. The Ascension, as I understood it as a child, was basically a disaster. Jesus went away to be with the Father, and now we had to live without his tangible presence until the end of time. The Ascension was the Feast of the Absence of God, or the Festival of the Divine Abandonment. In today's Gospel (Jn 16:16–20), the apostles respond as I once did. Jesus is trying to tell them about his death and Resurrection, but as yet they just can't get the message. All they get is that he is going away, and they can't understand why. All they really understand is that they don't understand. "We do not know what he means," they lament, and they're afraid even to ask him to explain (18).

I was afraid in youth to ask as well. To inquire about the absence of God seems to many in the Church to suggest atheism—which, indeed, is how my religious educators took it when as a teen I started asking difficult questions about all the ways in which God seems to be missing from the world. It was the 1980s, and my mind was full of eighties crises, such as AIDS, Ethiopian famine, the Cold War, and the nuclear arms race. The result: I started to get thrown out of Sunday school on a regular basis. And not long after that, I started to think of myself as an agnostic. It's a small step from the claim that God was here once (*two thousand* years ago!) and will return (but only long after I'm gone!) to the simpler, more direct conclusion that God was never here at all. And in a way, how can one blame the disciples? Whom do you ask about the absence of God? Who can explain what it means? It's paradoxical to ask God, and who else could answer the question?

Cynewulf's "Christ" poem, however, depicts the Ascension as the ultimate triumph, as the ultimate guarantor of meaning. How could we really hope to be taken into heaven if Christ didn't go there himself? Perhaps even more important, how could God be the true guarantor of meaning if the realm of the divine wasn't the ultimate source of all earthly meaning? In the Ascension, Jesus' real, material body is caught up into God. And Cynewulf explains that it is there that we must then find our hope, and thus that we must understand the world in which we live, reading it in light of heaven; we must never become attached to the things of earth as ends in themselves, detached from divine meaning. The Ascension is both the guarantee that the world has meaning and a check on any tendency to make the material world an idol. So in typical graduate school fashion, I went and wrote a paper about Neoplatonism, Augustinian thought, and Anglo-Saxon poetry. True enough so far as it went, if a bit pretentious.

But I couldn't write for class about what I really saw in the poem, and what I had really learned, though for the first time I understood why the Ascension mattered and why anyone would want to celebrate it.

On earth, not in heaven, discussions about houses and where our family should live continue. As Emily and I sit down on the living-room sofa to start our evening adult conversation over coffee, I fear that I can predict her words. She will with unconscious irony echo the words of Jesus (Jn 14:2–3): she has prepared a mansion for me, that where she longs to be, there I may be also. I brace myself to hear about the latest Victorian with cedar shake shingles.

But I've actually read her completely wrong. "So let's say we stay here," she begins. I can hardly process what I'm hearing. "If we're really serious about our treasure being in heaven, not on earth," she says, "maybe our money should be invested in other people, not real estate. If we stay here, we could do a lot more for the poor—and for Beatrice. Just a thought. Just maybe. But it's worth thinking about." Then she goes back to sipping her coffee. I'm sufficiently startled that I don't have much to say in return; I'm afraid to break the spell.

I still don't know what we'll end up doing; this discussion is obviously far from finished. But it's good to remember as I write these ruminations that I'm not the only one reflecting on the liturgy—Emily is doing the readings every day as well—and that the Church is not bestowing her wisdom on me alone. Just when I'm feeling particularly holy and superior, the tables are turned on me.

Monday of the Seventh Week of Easter (Jn 16:29–33)

Emily is wondering today if she is pregnant. "You know," she said this morning as we were getting dressed and ready to face the day, "I'm thinking I might not have the flu after all."

I knew immediately where we were going. Just as quickly, I knew that the openness to life and God and generation that I professed on the Feast of the Annunciation was a forced pious sentiment. I feel neither trust nor faith nor joy. I feel only panic. I don't—as I should—imagine the irreplaceably unique young life we would be ushering into the world. I imagine only the life Emily and I have carefully created collapsing in slow motion. Right now, our free time is minimal (and just returning!) and sleep diminished, but we are managing; everything still functions, albeit by a razor's edge. But in an expanding family, the complicated juggling act by which we manage our jobs and our commitments—to church, to friends, to each other—will simply go to pot. And something—perhaps me, perhaps Beatrice, perhaps my relationship with my wife, perhaps whatever individual hopes or ambitions Emily and I still harbor unspoken—will get thrown and dropped. I begin imagining our future: a montage of scenes of disaster and recrimination (some plagiarized from my parents' marriage, some entirely original).

But then I breathe deeply and catch myself. The voice of panic is never the voice of God. God knows what he's doing. If there is anything we've learned over the last number of years, it's that we need always to have an openness to the work of God, who is often acting in ways that we cannot imagine. The complications of having a second child are obvious. Children are, by definition, unmanageable; they will thwart any scheme of careful organization and take your life in directions in which you did not intend it to go. And, at least for me, the blessings of having a child aren't really imaginable without seeing the child.

Children are individual souls, not a collective mass. I love my daughter intensely and appreciate every way in which she has altered my life, but the general idea of children does not stir me in perhaps the way it should.

On the other hand, Emily just turned thirty-five, and I'll be forty in the fall. If a child were born today, I would be pushing retirement age when he graduated from college. If we wait until Emily is menopausal to be open to God, how open are we really? How, then, do we differ from our secular friends who openly worship barrenness and personal convenience? Perhaps only in that our secular friends are more honest with themselves and the world.

As I've mentioned, Emily's been doing the liturgical readings with me this year. One effect of doing these readings is that you begin to realize you're part of a larger story, the story of the Church, of the Kingdom of God, whose next move you don't know and in which you're not always sure of your role. If Emily is pregnant, this wouldn't be the next chapter we would have imagined, but we wouldn't have imagined our present lives in the first place either, so that doesn't tell us much. Clinging to the present moment is an act of unbelief and arrogance.

The Gospel today (Jn 16:29–33) speaks of God's provision: "I have told you this so that you might have peace in me. In the world you will have trouble, but take courage, I have conquered the world" (33). When we trust in God, we are affirming life and believing that the fundamental principle of reality is neither money nor power. We are affirming that, as Emily—yes, unthinkably, Emily, the obsessive planner who literally arranges her life on a spreadsheet—observed today, "Life's not something we really should try to conquer and govern on our own terms. That would make sense only if we understood life—and we don't. But maybe our lives *could* be a holy chaos where God can move."

Perhaps part of this liturgical year is learning this story.

Tuesday of the Seventh Week of Easter
(Acts 20:17–27)

Emily is still wondering if she is pregnant, and this dominated our conversation last night on a long walk–stroller ride through our generally 1970s split-level or brick ranch subdivision. As we pushed Beatrice past ranch house after ranch house, and purely decorative split rail fence after split rail fence, we tried to think through the logistics of multichild life. Could the kids get on the same sleep schedule? Could Beatrice go to an all-day Christian preschool (she would be about three) while we juggle our work schedules—and employ some grandparental help—to care for the new child? Could we abandon the strict breast-milk program we had followed with Beatrice (which was quite difficult) and give the new child any liquid he is capable of ingesting?[3]

As we dodged cars and drifted downhill on the busier second half of the walk, we also tried without success to figure out how a pregnancy would affect matters we have already been discussing. Does a child mean that we need to move into a bigger home quickly? Or that we need to stay where we are to save money? Basically, we went round and round in frantic circles.

Then, stroller put away and child put to bed, we looked at houses on the Internet. Then we got sleepy and silly

---

[3] Note to advocates of breast feeding and opponents of all-day preschool: Don't worry. These things will not ultimately happen.

and began employing an online random baby-name generator. Suggested boys' names: Soren, Yuvra, and Enrique. Suggested girls' names: Flick, Aneesa, and Audrey. Then terrible insomnia followed all around.

We also discussed the possibility that Emily's condition could be due not to pregnancy but to some very odd food we got Saturday from the Vietnamese restaurant next to the Big Lots discount store in a failing strip mall. We were the only customers in the restaurant the whole time we were there. Incense burned before idols; the eyes of animals floated in the soup; reruns of *How I Met Your Mother* blared on an unwatched TV so loudly that it was impossible to think. The scene seemed both surreal and forlorn. And, though Beatrice seems fine, I've been feeling like I could be pregnant ever since that meal as well.

"I feel like I have a tapeworm. It would be strange if all this were just due to a Vietnamese tapeworm," Emily remarked this morning.

"Then we'd have to name the tapeworm," I added, thinking back to the random baby-name generator, still sleepy and silly. "What do you name a Vietnamese tapeworm?"

She suggested, "Tet," and I guessed correctly that she was making a somewhat shameless Vietnam War pun. The Tet Offensive was a major campaign in the Vietnam War and, yes, a tapeworm is "offensive".

So we wait to see whether Emily is bearing a tapeworm named Tet or a girl possibly named Gertrude Katherine. And we have now admitted that we're both terrified of making the adjustments involved in having another child and that we would also be sort of disappointed if there was no pregnancy. Perhaps if this all does turn out to be a false alarm—Emily was carefully following Natural Family Planning, and it's worked for many years without a hitch—God is using the whole silly incident to get us thinking about something we should have been doing anyway. We need such harassment to think sanely and to act in holiness.

In today's reading from Acts (Acts 20:17–27), Paul closes by saying, "I did not shrink from proclaiming to you the entire plan of God" (27). Neither do his successors, the present bishops of the Catholic Church. Despite all pressure to the contrary, the Church will not cease to proclaim what once was obvious: that sex is oriented toward procreation; that it's good to bring life into the world; that true love is generative; that we shouldn't live closed off, hermetically sealed lives that we can perfectly control.

My wife and I are Americans and, worse, professors. As I've already admitted, we wouldn't have had children at all if the Church hadn't made us promise prior to the wedding that we were open to children and if we weren't honest enough to follow her logic. Left to ourselves, we would like lives that are closed off, are carefully contained, are crafted exactly to our specifications, and culminate in leisure. For us, leisure means classical music and trips to Europe; for you, it might mean jet skis and Disney World, but there is no real moral difference. Virtually all Americans embody Oscar Wilde's dictum from *The Picture of Dorian Gray*: "We live in an age where unnecessary things are our only necessities." Yes, sadly, in a state of nature we—and probably you—are that kind of people. We are saved from our antiseptic selves by the Church proclaiming the entire plan of God—even the parts that we would rather leave out.

5

THE HARD ART OF REMEMBERING
(Ordinary Time, Round 2, Part 1)

Monday of the Eighth Week in Ordinary Time
(Mk 10:17–27)

Emily and I spent our early years of marriage as graduate students living below the federal poverty line. Although we accepted no government assistance ourselves, we rented an apartment in a Section 8 complex, since it had the lowest rates around. The complex had its peculiarities: a four-year-old boy named John Wayne wandered the streets clad only in a diaper, our next-door neighbors dealt methamphetamines, and water from a burst pipe (never repaired) seeped up through our living-room floor. And life had its difficulties: each month, we barely made the rent, and every car breakdown constituted a potentially unsolvable crisis. For me, living hand-to-mouth wasn't a new experience; as I've mentioned, after my father left my mother, my family took a quick trip into downward mobility. And except for the geyser in our living room, I liked our apartment complex; the rent was low, John Wayne was a friendly enough kid, and the next-door neighbors were, for obvious reasons, the most wonderfully quiet I ever had. Subsistence living was more of an adjustment for Emily, but she did adjust, learning to cook excellent meals that were basically free and managing our budget to stretch every dollar.

So it's confusing that we now find ourselves solidly middle class, dealing with an ethical problem we never expected to face: how to use wealth appropriately. When you decide to major in the liberal arts in college, you figure you'll never have to worry about what you would have done with the money you'll never earn. But, somehow, here we are.

We give to the Church and at least theoretically recognize that nothing we have is really our own; it all belongs to God. But we begin to be faced with middle-class questions. My wife finds herself again wanting a bigger house in a nicer neighborhood. Is that ethically acceptable? Is having a bigger house acceptable at all? What most of the world's population calls a house Americans call a garden shed, and Emily and I already have enough space to get by as is (about fifteen hundred square feet). Is the idea of moving into a nicer neighborhood a commendable part of the American Dream, or does it amount to an elitist desire to cordon yourself off from anyone who is suffering or struggling? If you buy a nice house, are you giving your child a better life, or are you pillaging her college fund? And these questions become only more confusing if you start to evaluate them in comparative terms. For me, a $350,000 house is the height of folly; my mother's house was worth $80,000 in its prime and now, after Detroit's real estate collapse, would likely go for half that. You could probably buy her *block* for $350,000.[1] But my wife might consider a $350,000 house to be frugal, because people in her field (university administration) often have $500,000 houses.

We're trying to think hard about what's ethically acceptable in this case for a family of three (Emily turned

[1] My mother, who is proud of her neighborhood, would want you to know that real estate values in her area have since recovered.

out not to be pregnant; we found out Monday). It's hard to get guidance, since (apart from a few near Franciscans) even in Christian circles, the response to our questions simply seems to be, "You've earned it with all those years in graduate school; spend it."

But the liturgical year tells us otherwise. Emily came home from work this afternoon, excitedly talking about ideas for the new house that she now wants to build out in the country. As she was changing clothes in our upstairs bedroom from dress suit into T-shirt and shorts, she laid out her case. "I want an exact replica of my grandparents' house in Ohio. My great-grandfather designed it and built it. It was beautiful, and it used space efficiently. It would look right in Virginia. I've found some great lots not far from here. And I've got the names of a couple of good contractors."

I didn't even have the courage to look at her. I made myself busy getting something out of the nightstand and replied without looking up. "In the Mass readings, today's Gospel was the rich young ruler [Mk 10:17–27]."

I didn't need to say anything more. Emily knows her Bible all too well and could automatically fill in the blanks: Jesus tells a pious and sincere young man who wishes to be a disciple, "Go; sell what you have, and give to the poor, and you will have treasure in heaven; then come, follow me" (21). The young man walks away sad, prompting Jesus' famous remark, "How hard it is for those who have wealth to enter the Kingdom of God. It is easier for a camel to pass through the eye of a needle than for one who is rich to enter into the Kingdom of God" (24–25).

Emily put her earrings down and leaned against the dresser. Then she turned to face me, threw up her hands, and dramatically sighed, "Should we just stay here?"

The liturgical year is becoming a third voice in all our discussions, a not-always-welcome voice of wisdom, butting in with insights we didn't necessarily want to hear. Its timing is also increasingly eerie; the liturgical year seems to be developing an uncanny ability to predict our lives.

But, unless like Saint Francis we take the story of the rich young ruler as a personal injunction and immediately sell all we have and give to the poor, we're still left with the ethical question unresolved. Beyond some very broad general guidelines—like "support the Church" and "help the poor"—the Church offers no clear and definitive teaching on the issue. So how do you know what is ethically right? Well, if you're a traditionalist, you study the lives of the saints. If you're a charismatic, you enter into prayer in the Spirit. But if you're geeky college professors, you interview a panel of broadly representative experts. So that's what we decided to do: we chose one Catholic priest (for obvious reasons), one well-respected theologian (since we're theoretical sorts), and one Protestant minister (as a nod to ecumenism).

Tuesday of the Eighth Week in Ordinary Time
(1 Pet 1:10–16)

Saint Peter today (1 Pet 1:10–16, the second reading) tells us that we need to be trained for heaven. We need to be conditioned to live the spiritual life. This could seem paradoxical. If God made us for heaven and for the things of the spirit, how can they seem foreign to us?

Heaven is our ultimate end, but as fallen creatures we don't simply take to it naturally. We have to change our mental hard wiring, so that we no longer think and feel according to "the desires of [our] former ignorance" (14). Physical strength is perhaps an analogy here. We naturally possess a potentiality for physical strength, but unless we activate it through a rigorous (and by no means natural or intuitive) process of training, it will never be actuated. I know that I certainly never have actuated whatever physical strength I possess and that exercise never ceased to feel weird, foreign, and basically stupid and boring to me. Exercise is thus at once supremely natural and entirely artificial. Peter asks us to imagine the spiritual disciplines in similar terms, as types of training by which we may "gird up the loins of [our] mind" (13). By awkwardly doing the same thing over and over, a person gradually becomes natural at it and even develops muscle memory so that it feels wrong *not* to do it. We habituate ourselves into the life of the spirit; we acculturate ourselves into heaven.

As banal as it is, and as scatological as it sounds, the biggest event in my life in recent weeks has been potty training Beatrice. It's hard to figure out how one learns— or teaches—an automatic process. Beatrice runs pantless through the house yelling, "I don't want to sit on the potty!" Then Beatrice misses her pink princess potty and poops on the ceramic tile. Finally, she sits on the potty— but produces no material product.

Yet, once Emily institutes a program in which every time Beatrice potties successfully, she receives a sticker to place on a piece of pink construction paper taped over the toilet, everything suddenly changes. As an added incentive, we also decide to give her an M&M—in the color of her choice—each time. "Bea did it! Yeah for Bea!" Bea now yells. And we reinforce the result with a weird little call and response:

"Who pottied on the potty?"
"Bea pottied on the potty."
"Who's gonna get a sticker?"
"Bea's gonna get a sticker."
"Who's gonna get some candy?"
"Bea's gonna get some candy."

This is an apt, if degrading, analogy for the spiritual life. God blesses us in external ways that we can comprehend—job, spouse, friends, and so on—to reach us where we're at by talking to us in our own terms. We need tangible blessings so we can begin to want to internalize what God is teaching us, even before we fully share his values. But the goal is to end up entirely elsewhere, somewhere where those terms would be without meaning. The real rewards are those which in our current frame of reference we couldn't even conceive. As in the case of the potty training, the real goal is for Beatrice to become, in the most rudimentary of senses, a self-controlled adult. But that has no meaning for her at present. Hence, stickers. Hence, everything we consider most important in our lives at present.

Wednesday of the Eighth Week in Ordinary Time
(Mk 10:32–45)

Our panelists' schedules couldn't be reconciled, so we're now consulting them individually. Today we met with our first panelist, a friend who is a Nazarene pastor with a master's degree in divinity. Emily said in advance of the meeting, "He's just going to say that we have to pray, and I hate that."

He is a jovial fellow whose idea of formal wear is a polo shirt and khakis and whose facial hair is continually advancing and retreating between goatee and beard. He is comfortable in his own skin and seems to take no notice of his own appearance. He is ecumenical by nature, and his theological training possesses a Catholic inflection—too much of a Catholic inflection for some: the now-former president of his college was the sole Nazarene signatory of the "Evangelicals and Catholics Together" statement which proposed that, while retaining our theological distinctives, we should work together to transform a secular culture for Christ. Graduates of the college are blackballed in some Evangelical quarters. Our Nazarene pastor friend is full of the sense that the Gospel really does have all the answers for the world in which we live, if only we didn't limit so radically what it was allowed to say. Emily and I are talking to him because he may be the most sincere and unaffected person we know. If he felt like God was telling him to go live in the woods, he would be among the trees—with his wife and three kids in tow—no questions asked.

We stepped into his office in a converted ranch house, he made us coffee out of a Keurig, and we all sat down and hashed things out. He introduced a theory of self-sacrificial giving, by saying, with an ironic nod of the head, "I didn't actually live this out, but I read in a book that—"

"Who do you think you're talking to?" I cut him off. "I've always preferred books to real life. What did it say?"

So our pastor friend quoted John Wesley's sermon on wealth and poverty. Wesley, we learned, held that everything you don't absolutely need belongs by right to the poor (a position that his wife did not greatly appreciate). Wesley made a fortune on his book publications and gave it all away. His detestation of wealth was so extreme that he banned even art and nice clothing from his house as luxuries and, so far as he was concerned, vices.

Then our friend digressed and wondered aloud, "Do I really need a house at all when people are living in sewers?" He told us that he feels that the question of what to do about money is in some ways the key issue for the Church today. And then, as Emily had predicted, without

giving us any absolute answers, he told us that we have
to pray.

But more informatively, he gave us some ideas about
the direction in which to pray. He suggested that how you
should spend your money is tied to your "personal mission". The service of God is not abstract, he explained. We
serve an incarnate God who wishes to help real, specific
people with their real, specific problems. You don't give
away money just to get rid of it or keep it just to keep it.
Money is a tool to serve a mission. He suggested that we
begin praying as a family to have a collective sense of vocation, some idea of what God would have us do next, what
task we should take on for the Kingdom together. If we
knew that, we might know where and how we should live.

Finally, our friend said, "Would you be comfortable if
I led us all in a word of prayer?" We gathered around the
Keurig to pray; he led us in a prayer that was as heartfelt as
the setting was ridiculous, and then we went on our way.

In the Gospel today (Mk 10:32–45), James and John
seek high positions in Christ's Kingdom; they wish to sit
at his right and left hand, which is to say, they wish to be
his number-one and number-two lieutenants in ruling
the redeemed world. Jesus responds, "Whoever wishes to
be great among you will be your servant; whoever wishes
to be first among you will be the slave of all. For the Son
of Man did not come to be served but to serve and to give
his life as a ransom for many" (43–45). The liturgical year
perhaps anticipates our conversation today. Like James
and John, we are making the wrong request and asking
the wrong questions. We wonder what kind of house we
should have and what sort of possessions we should own
relative to our economic position. Jesus says we should be
asking instead how we should serve; make that the first
priority, and everything else will fall into place.

Solemnity of the Most Holy Trinity (Mt 28:16–20)

Today Emily was ill and stayed home from Mass, so I watched Beatrice solo at church. To keep my daughter from freaking out, I threw a different means of entertainment at her every few seconds. Board book about Jesus? Stuffed rabbit? Cup of milk? Crayons with paper? Dried cranberries? Still, she kept standing on the seat of the pew and peering over the top, trying to make conversation with the people behind me. Mercifully, they were egging her on rather than rolling their eyes. She showed them the bow in her hair, her stuffed animal, everything except the dried cranberries.

I've been trying to teach her about the parts of the Mass, but she hasn't yet learned to whisper. So she bellowed out key moments like a radio baseball announcer:

"This is the Gos-pel."

"Father pray-ing."

"There's the shopping cart. Food for hungry people."

She did very well for a two-year-old, making it all through Mass, but I left entirely harried and unrecollected, feeling that the service had passed me by unawares.

The homily at Mass was about the Trinity as society, about how God in his undivided nature is not solitary and alone but constitutes a community; there is an interplay of love that exists before the universe and is reflected in the universe, and we exist only in and through that love. Our ideal and origin, then, is not the protective seclusion of isolation (whether that of a solitary God or an empty universe) but the free exchange of love and gift. The priest's point was that the Trinity is not simply an abstract theological proposition or an unfathomable mystery (though it is both). The Trinity tells us who we are and what sort of world we're living in. It is a guide to life; the Gospel reading (Mt 28:16–20) explicitly connects the idea of the Trinity to our concrete Christian lives; through baptism, we enter the community "of the Father, and of the Son, and of the Holy Spirit" (19).

The homily and readings, then, put my Mass experience into perspective. Rather than mourning my failure to attain a state of solitary contemplation, I should be happy that I have the opportunity to welcome my daughter into the community of the Church, to have her become part of this divine society, to have her learn with me to become part of the life of God, as it is expressed in this community. She loves, especially, the parts of Mass where the community is most evident. She barks out with particular joy, "Those the greeters", "We hold hands and pray", and "We shake hands and say, 'Peace be with you.'" She is sharing in Christ's peace. And all of this is far more important than whether I attain the state of contemplative abstraction that I desire.

Wednesday of the Ninth Week in Ordinary Time
(2 Tim 1:1–3, 6–12)

We had the pastor of our parish over for dinner last night. If one has a theological question to work through, the obvious place to turn is to one's parish priest. Our second panelist is a bearded, hefty man about sixty years old, with short, graying dark hair and glasses. More to the point, he is deeply sardonic, and he is always in character. So naturally, he wore a green Hawaiian shirt rather than clericals, laughed nervously at his own jokes, complained about the new Mass translation ("How are we supposed to say that? We're all children of Ernest Hemingway and the short, declarative sentence, like it or not"), and sprinkled his insightful practical advice with recycled lines from late-night comedian Stephen Colbert.

But today's epistle reading is 2 Timothy 1:1–3, 6–12. Our pastor may not be tailored to suit my theological or liturgical preferences, but he still possesses "the gift of God ... through the imposition of [the] hands" of the bishop; something transcendent has taken place in him (6). And, somehow, wise counsel out of the heart of the Catholic tradition came tonight along with that Hawaiian shirt. He took in our situation—do you sell all you have and give to the poor or buy a McMansion?—and immediately began the great Catholic practice of making precise distinctions. The relevant distinction, he explained, is between acts of justice and acts of charity.

Giving a tithe is an act of justice, to support the community of faith to which you belong. Providing for parents and children is also an act of justice, a duty that you owe them. We had wondered if we should get a bigger house in case my wife's parents later need to live with us. He spoke with the practicality of a confessor, suggesting that instead of working everything out in theory in our heads we get outside of ourselves and actually talk to *them* about what *they* would want or need. They've moved down here, they help with our daughter, we're close to them, they're an integral part of our daily lives—if it would make them feel better or more secure to know they had a place with us in the future, we should consider that in where we live and how we live. If, on the other hand, they desperately wish to be independent of us, we shouldn't impose a residence on them just so we can think well of ourselves and our ethics. "My mother would rather have *died* than live with me," he candidly added.

When acts of justice are taken care of, then you move on to acts of charity. He suggested giving as much as we can to a few organizations whose work we trust and that we know do good work for people, and giving to them consistently. We should also be giving our time to these ministries.

And then he drove his Japanese subcompact off into the night, leaving us with much to think about, not least his own vocation. It's easy to be dismissive of the local priest and to idealize distant clerics who might be more according to one's own tastes. But he has given himself fully to God in a way that I have not, and the gift will not fail; the gift will out.

Solemnity of the Most Holy Body and Blood of Christ (Corpus Christi) (Mk 14:12–16, 22–26)

Today is the Feast of Corpus Christi. Citing the Gospel reading (Mk 14:12–16, 22–26), the priest in his homily made the feast not merely a celebration but an ethical imperative. We don't just receive the Blood of Christ; we receive Christ's "blood of the covenant, which will be shed for many" (24). If we are to celebrate and consume the Body and Blood of Christ poured out for us at Mass, we must also become the body of Christ in our lives for the world and must pour ourselves out for others. He connected this idea to our service to family, neighbors, the parish community, and even our willingness, when we are weak, to surrender our dignity by allowing others to help us. Since Christ comes to us in his lowliness, the test of our sincerity in receiving the sacrament—the test of whether we really believe that what is taking place is the height of human meaning—is our willingness to hold ourselves lightly, to lower and abase ourselves for others.

And I think here I fail in basically all my relations. I treat my wife well—I am polite, self-controlled, and deferential—but everything is painstakingly negotiated (I'll cover this chore if she'll cover that; I can agree to moving if she makes these concessions; etc.). Am I really ready to be poured out for her? For Beatrice? For my family? For my wife's family? For my students? My colleagues? The world?

Or do I secretly think that it was the ancient Greek philosopher Epicurus who gave his life for me, so that I might live on Epicurean terms, by means of a strict rational calculation of self-interested pleasure? Epicurus—unlike many people who call themselves epicures—realized that ideas last longer than things, and the temperate life is more likely to give pleasure than the life of excess. Since prudence and moderation are also Christian virtues, a quiet life lived for Epicurus and a quiet life lived for Christ can deceptively mirror each other. The Feast of Corpus Christi makes me wonder where I've really sought a savior.

Feast of Saint Barnabas, Apostle (June 11)
(Acts 11:21b–26; 13:1–3; Mt 10:7–13)

Yesterday, in addition to Mass, I found myself attending a service at an Evangelical Protestant church to which I have many connections. The pastor is a short, hyperenergetic former high school basketball and tennis coach who keeps his graying hair cropped short and wears trendy square plastic glasses. Unsurprisingly, his forte is the motivational lecture. In the liturgical year of his own devising, it was the feast of "Kids Matter Sunday", so he gave an inspirational sermon about mentors, using Paul and Timothy as examples. "Everybody needs a Paul in his life," he said, "and everybody needs a Timothy." Many heartwarming stories followed, of children previously without adult figures—especially male adult figures—in their lives who were transformed because of a "Paul" who stepped in and guided them spiritually and personally. Most of the stories involved sports. All led to the same basic point: everyone should run off and find a kid to mentor.

His message isn't without truth. Only a terrible person could object to encouraging adults to help youth. But I *am* a terrible person, so I found myself declaring him guilty of oversimplifying both the Bible and human life. I hadn't looked ahead in the Catholic missal, and didn't know that today was the Feast of Saint Barnabas, but I asked my wife over lunch, "Why do you never hear a sermon about how every Paul needs a Barnabas and every Barnabas needs a Paul?"—meaning, you need a friend who helps you develop into the person you are going to be, from whom you later become estranged and to whom you fail to speak for decades.

"A frenemy," Emily added.

"Exactly," I said, beginning to parody the sermon. "So many people tragically look outside the Church for their frenemies, when there are plenty of people who feel called to be their frenemies—who would be more than willing to be their frenemies—right here in the house of God." For that's basically the story of Paul and Barnabas, and it suggests that there is no one biblical model of the role other people should play in your spiritual development.

Barnabas and Paul were the original missionaries to the Gentiles, called by the Holy Spirit. As the epistle reading (Acts 11:21b–26; 13:1–3) records, "The Holy Spirit said, 'Set apart for me Barnabas and Saul for the work to which I have called them'" (13:2). Thus it was that Paul's amazingly successful missionary journeys began. But later Paul ended up feeling that their assistant Mark was unreliable, Barnabas defended Mark, and the whole Paul-Barnabas missionary project broke up over this, like the John Lennon–Paul McCartney songwriting team over Yoko Ono. The striking thing is that the Bible seems to condemn neither Paul nor Barnabas for their long break. It seems to be just one of those things that nothing could be done about, one of those differences of opinion that simply couldn't be resolved, and no one seems to bear moral fault in the matter. The Bible is so much more complicated, and so much truer to life, than our motivational sermons.

As far as I can parse it, the story of Paul and Barnabas teaches us that the truly important thing is the Kingdom of God itself and that our personal friendships are really quite secondary. Barnabas and Paul were never malicious with each other, and Paul never accuses Barnabas of undermining his ministry (a charge he is more than willing to make against others); they just can't agree and have to part ways. As it turns out, it's best that they do so; their parting becomes a means of fulfilling Jesus' injunction to proclaim to the world, "The Kingdom of heaven is at hand" (which happens to be the first verse of today's Gospel, Mt 10:7–13). Paul and Barnabas' missionary reach is doubled, as Mark and Barnabas go off on one set of missionary journeys and Paul and Silas on another.

As Christians, we try to work problems out with each other, and try to be compassionate and generous, but the result is always in the hands of God. We have to accept the uncertainty and contingency of life and the freedom of other people's wills and that we live in a complicated world where even the well-meaning won't always see sufficiently eye to eye to stand each other. The Feast of Saint Barnabas reminds us that God understands this situation, even if we don't, and God can use such unlikely circumstances as means of redemption. God is the Lord of the universe, not a motivational speaker.

Eleventh Sunday in Ordinary Time (Mk 4:26–34)

In the secular calendar, today is Father's Day. I grew up with Evangelical Protestant Father's Day sermons and still approach church on this day with fear, though (save for a final blessing) it has been my experience that Catholic services for the most part ignore the holiday. Evangelical Father's Day sermons typically offer a simple equation of earthly parentage with divine parentage; you learn who God is by honoring your father, and by being a father you occupy what my brother, a good man and a devoted father, quite seriously refers to as "the earthly God role".

In my upbringing—and this is by no means unique to Protestants—there is also an assumption that as a parent you control how your children turn out. If you do things right, then your children are guaranteed to turn out well. "Raise up a child in the way he should go, and when he is old he will not depart from it" (Prov 22:6).

All of this is well intended and supposed to be encouraging, but it is ultimately depressing. How could you ever plan your child's life sufficiently to guarantee a positive result? When the child doesn't do what is desired, is the parent guilty of poor planning? In short, who could be fit to be an "earthly God"? (There are good reasons why we don't have earthly gods; they're called "idols".)

If I believed in these types of Father's Day sermons, I couldn't stand to be a father at all. Yesterday, Beatrice carefully removed her diaper and deliberately peed all over her crib not once but twice. Is this because I'm not a fit earthly God? If I sounded rather cross with her since she urinated all over the blankets, does this mean that she'll grow up to be a traumatized, estranged, and immoral person? Or, alternately, will she grow up to be a wild and amoral person because when confronted with something like a urine-soaked bed I tend to be rather soft and use very little discipline (at most, I might sound a little cross)? There is no good outcome to this line of reasoning.

My great consolation as a father is that God's fatherhood is in no way dependent on my own. I'm sure I'll make a million mistakes in raising my daughter, but if I introduce her to God, and she chooses to follow God, she'll have a reliable guide in her life. My parents are well-meaning people, but in my teenage years (the years when a person's adult identity is set), my father was often absent and unaccounted for through days or weeks on end, and my mother (understandably) grappled with depression. Still, my parents, however imperfectly they may have behaved, raised us in church and with knowledge of God and Scripture. And my siblings and I are all now God-fearing, productive members of society. There is no one-to-one relation between parental behavior and the adult a child becomes; free will gets in the way. And this is a real solace. I can try to do my best by my daughter, but I don't have to play God. I can introduce her to God and leave him to play that role.

My wife finds my feelings about Father's Day rather extreme. She observes as we drink coffee at the dining-room table, "The Bible does call God a Father, you know, and people do have more trouble relating to God as a father if, ahem, they have difficulty relating to their fathers." (That hits home. For although in many ways I admire my father, I know that I have never really understood him. Where another man would merely lust, my father commits adultery. Where another man would just give a vagrant a buck and pass him by, my father invites him back home. He is equally intemperate in vice and virtue. Neither his strengths nor his weaknesses are my own.)

For a moment, I cannot help but concede. "Of course, that's true. That's Saint Thomas Aquinas' analogy of being; all created things tell us something about the Creator." But I know I'm not going to let the point drop. I look out the window and recall that today's Gospel was the parable of the mustard seed (Mk 4:26–34); in the children's Liturgy of the Word, the teacher had passed out seeds to all the children. I find my theme and continue. "All created things tell us something about the Creator. So, according to the Thomistic analogy of being, the tree outside our window would also tell me something about the nature of God if I could read it aright. And doubtless, modern urbanized people have more trouble relating to God as a Creator since they don't get the Bible's agricultural metaphors. But I don't have to put up with over-the-top holidays about horticulture."

Of course, I was overdoing it, and overstating my case (as usual; she had struck a nerve). But neither was I entirely wrong. The Bible shows us many ways to look at God, all containing valuable insights. Particularly, God's immanence (his Fatherhood) and his transcendence (dwelling in "inaccessible light") both need to be taken into account. As far as holidays go, we've got immanence covered. So what about a holiday named after Saint Anselm's title for God—"that than which nothing greater can be thought"? I could get behind that.

It might be difficult to invite the relatives over ("Hey, you coming over for 'That Than Which Nothing Greater Can Be Thought' Day? Great. What time?"). I can also imagine Emily's complaints ("What am I supposed to cook for 'That Than Which Nothing Greater Can Be Thought' Day? I mean, that's setting the bar a bit high. No pressure there.") But, to be sure we have both sides of the paradox covered, why not give the new holiday a try?

Wednesday of the Eleventh Week in Ordinary Time
(Mt 6:1–6, 16–18)

In today's Gospel (Mt 6:1–6, 16–18), Jesus tells us that when we "perform righteous deeds", "give alms", "pray", or "fast", we should act in secret so that our only audience is God (1, 2, 4, 6). Only if we avoid being seen by people will our "Father who sees in secret" reward us (6). I always wonder exactly what to do with Jesus' remarks. On the one hand, yes, existential legitimacy means that we must each stand alone before God. Before God, all absurdity and pretense are stripped away and each person simply is what he is. Unless a person is generous and self-giving when alone before God, a person has no real charity.

On the other hand, Jesus' remarks are predicated on a cultural background in which religious observance and deeds of charity are valued and affirmed. And we no longer live in such a culture. Certainly, to many of my colleagues, I would seem more credible as a scholar of religion and literature if I did not attend Mass (adherence to a particular religion can be taken as a sin against academic objectivity). And college students, the other group of people with which I am most regularly in contact, all too often view chastity and sobriety as discreditable weaknesses. In a creative-writing course I recently taught, my female students spent the minutes before class loudly narrating to each other what it's like to have sex on top of the washing machine in the dorm's public laundry room, while my male students described in equal detail how they managed to elude the police after drunkenly defacing public property. The students who were chaste and sober remained quiet about it, probably less out of humility than out of embarassment. As G. K. Chesterton quipped in *The Paradoxes of Mr. Pond*, the old maxim has been reversed—hypocrisy is now the homage that virtue pays to vice.[2]

To turn to less R-rated topics, in the Church no one talks about how much money he gives away to the poor (that would be bragging, letting the left hand know what the right hand is doing), but no one is ashamed to show off a McMansion or an investment portfolio (which somehow is acceptable). In my native Michigan, billionaire pizza baron Tom Monaghan was treated favorably in the press when he was amassing a fortune or building the world's largest private Frank Lloyd Wright collection; the press turned against him precisely when he began to give his fortune away to Catholic charities (he was now a "bigoted fanatic"). In short, the behavior Jesus describes in the Gospel will no longer cause you to receive "the praise of others" and the "reward" of increased status (cf. Mt 6:2).

So are Christians making a mistake when, in their sincere attempts to follow the words of Christ, they remain quiet about their good deeds and acts of prayer? By hiding our prayer and almsgiving, are we accidentally reinforcing a culture of godless materialism, in which prayer and almsgiving seem absurd or unthinkable? May it be that at the present cultural moment, our good deeds will paradoxically be secret even if we perform them in public—because no one is capable of understanding what we are doing or saying? Is it now impossible for our good deeds

---

[2] Chesterton's passage may be worth quoting in full; it is even more relevant now than when it was written. His character Captain Gahagan offers the confession: "I was better than I seemed. But what did that mean, except the spiritual blasphemy that I wanted to seem worse than I was? What could it mean, except that, far worse than one who practised vice, I admired it? Yes, admired it in myself; even when it wasn't there. I was the new hypocrite; but mine was the homage that virtue pays to vice" (G.K. Chesterton, *The Paradoxes of Mr. Pond* [New York: Dodd, Mead, 1937], chapter VI).

to be performed in the sight of men, because all observers will misread and misinterpret our actions? The last time I volunteered at a soup kitchen, everyone I fed assumed I was there on community service for a public intoxication charge (the assumption had some statistical basis; in college towns, judicial order is the most common instigator of acts of virtue). My good deed was hidden even from the people for whom I performed it. If nothing we do can be conceived, we can hide in plain sight; we'll be alone with God even while parading in the crowd.

On June 9, we had the third of our panelists over for dinner. We had already tried the clerics, to see what pastoral perspective they might have to offer, so this time we sought an academic to give us a more theoretical point of view. We nabbed our town's most famous theologian. He has published over twenty-five books, spoken widely on Catholic and Protestant radio, and successfully debated prominent atheist philosophers. But, despite his accomplishments, he is still a person upon whom you can force a dinner invitation and who will be too polite to turn it down. He is a slightly stocky fellow in his early sixties who enunciates the nasal accents of my native Detroit at a prodigious speed. He sports the short but entirely untamed beard of an autoworker, which may also regionally mark him; my father used to grow the same beard each winter.

As he scarfed down chicken marsala and tossed the sauce in impressionistic patterns all over the tablecloth, he laid out an equally aggressive assault on Christian materialism. The Church's failure to hold people responsible for how they spend their money—a failure not seen in the early Church—is, he said, the great scandal of modern American Christianity. He then analyzed and probed the Christian silence on this issue in terms similar to those I've outlined above.

"Okay," we said, "we're with you." Which was fortunate—to be against him would be very unpleasant; he hits like a jovial bulldozer. "But what, exactly, should we do?"

He handed us a pile of books on the subject and disappeared into the night. What else should we have expected from a theologian?

Friday of the Eleventh Week in Ordinary Time (Mt 6:19–23)

In today's Gospel (Mt 6:19–23), Jesus teaches us not to "store up ... treasures on earth, where moth and decay destroy, and thieves break in and steal. But store up treasures in heaven.... For where your treasure is, there also will your heart be" (19–20). This particular teaching of Jesus comes up over and over again in the books of theology that our third panelist left us to read. So I had already been thinking about it when I encountered it as today's Gospel and the Church told me that I should meditate on it once more.

I can't seem to escape the end of this passage: "For where your treasure is, there also will your heart be." In Hebrew thought, "heart" does not mean "emotions"; it means something much closer to "will". Our will resides wherever our treasure is, wherever we truly place our value—however much we may try to hide this fact from ourselves and from all those around us. The idea is rendered most literally in George McDonald's story "The Giant's Heart". A giant hides his heart in an eagle's nest and so cannot be killed whatever anyone does to his body, since his soul simply isn't there. Our body may be lumbering through work, the grocery store, or even the responses at Mass, but our actual existence is hidden away elsewhere. We're only half present to those things that we have deemed only secondarily real.

It's all too easy to give everyday examples of this: the professor who feels that academic research is the only valuable part of his job and who sleepily mumbles his way through lecture staring at the clock; my eighth-grade science teacher, who just sat and showed filmstrips or videos every day of the year (no exaggeration) but who suddenly became animate, engaged, and intelligent if you asked him to play chess; the comatose assembly-line worker who struts all over the bar when it comes time for karaoke.

To give a less negative example, I worked my way through college laboring in fast-food restaurants (as I've mentioned before). A store manager tried at one point to get me to leave college and advance through the management ranks. While other employees did end up dropping out and becoming restaurant managers, I replied, "Are you insane? The main thing that keeps me going is the hope that someday I'll get out of here" (as a twenty-year-old, I was rather low on tact). The restaurant was a means for me, and I wouldn't consider it as an end. My heart was elsewhere. And, to my surprise, the store manager, for all her questionable recruiting tactics, understood. She had dropped out of college to care for her siblings, whom her alcoholic father wasn't feeding. She too knew where her heart resided (with her family).

Jesus' words are a challenge: Is heaven, the pure state of being with God, so real to me that all material things are unreal by comparison? So real, in fact, that I am to trade the material for what is unseen? Now, of course, Jesus isn't asking us, as some skeptics have alleged, to treat the material world as worthless. Jesus is simply showing us where meaning ultimately resides, and precisely how to value the material world. I was a better employee than most at the burger restaurant precisely because my work was given significance by the fact that it enabled me to pay my college tuition; my experience was invested with meaning precisely because I thought ultimate meaning was lodged elsewhere. My work participated in this meaning. And it's the same with the material world. If meaning is ultimately lodged with God, all else participates in this divine meaning. If my treasure is in heaven, I will fear neither poverty nor the tedium of daily routine, because both can be experiences that reflect the divine and point me to where my will should reside.

Wednesday of the Twelfth Week in Ordinary Time (2 Kings 22:8–13; 23:1–3)

However much I may intellectually believe that the world is perpetually charged with divine meaning and that God is always in control, my temperament runs in a different direction. By nature, I'm inclined to imagine the world's story as a simple one of decline and collapse. Evangelical premillennial Christianity raised me to think this way: the world falls in a death spiral until God simply has to snuff it out in what amounts to an act of euthanasia. I grew up watching apocalyptic movies—raptured people disappear, leaving their toothbrushes behind on the sink and bathrobes on the floor, as elsewhere the beast from Revelation rises to power—and looking at multicolored charts that outlined the order of the disasters that would befall humanity at the world's end. In fifth grade, I wrote an apocalyptic short story, replete with famine, pestilence, and blood running down the gutters of the streets (heaven only knows what my public school teachers thought). I also grew up in the 1980s, at the tail end of the period when nuclear war still seemed eminently possible; as a teen, I posted in my bedroom not sports paraphernalia but a huge picture of a charred landscape with the subscript "There is no defense against nuclear weapons."

To be fair, it's easy to subsume biblical narrative into these terms. Israel seems to go downhill from the moment of its founding (a narrative some Protestants project onto the Church), and the world can seem to go downhill from the Garden of Eden to the apocalypse by way of the Flood. But if you accept this overly simplistic narrative, it's all too easy to adopt a quietistic attitude toward the public sphere (why get involved in the world's problems when all your efforts will ultimately be futile in the end?). It's just as easy (as I've often found) to extend this story to your own personal life and to expect a slow moral and spiritual decline that begins with a vigorous youth and ends in a feeble death; the best you can spiritually hope for, then, is to tread water as best you can for as long as you can.

The first reading for today (2 Kings 22:8–13; 23:1–3) reminds us that Israel's story—and the world's—is actually far more complicated. Josiah, the most righteous king of Israel since David, actually rules near the *end* of the nation's existence, dying about twenty-five years before the Babylonian exile. During Josiah's reign, the high priest Hilkiah discovers in the temple the lost book of the Law (22:8). The king tears his clothes when he hears its words, and orders it read to the whole nation (22:11; 23:2). All Judah becomes rededicated to the covenant, and for Josiah's whole thirty-one-year reign, the nation, even at this late date, is as God would have it be.

God's truth is always being lost and always being redis-covered by both individuals and nations, and whenever people find it they have life. Like the liturgical year, human life is charged with meaning, but its progression is more circular than linear—and it is certainly not a linear march toward doom. It's all more delicate and uncertain than this. At any moment we could reclaim the life of God—the scroll is there, just waiting to be discovered; the Bible lies on the shelf unopened; the saints' days pass by unobserved—and at any moment it could be lost.

Thirteenth Sunday in Ordinary Time
(2 Cor 8:7, 9, 13–15)

This week our area was hit by a meteorological phenomenon known as a "derecho". I'm not entirely clear as to what the term means, but it has something to do with high, straight-line winds, and it knocked down a bunch of trees, smashed some houses, and took out basically the whole city's power grid. Most of the city—us included—spent many days without power. We spent the day in hours-long lines at the only fast-food place open, desperately searching for calories and coffee. Our pastor joined us in line for half an hour, at first making some jokes, then playing on his iPad, and finally disappearing, having decided that starvation was preferable.

The few churches that still had electricity kept their doors open all week to help anyone stuck out in the heat, and Father is letting anyone who wishes to sleep at the parish. But my wife and I, alas, have been too proud to take him up on the offer. I'm from the Upper Midwest, and I just can't adjust to the South without air-conditioning, so for me no power means no sleep. I've spent the nights sweating terribly, bothered over and over again by fireworks and a frightened dog (the Fourth of July draws near). But still, this morning we struggled out of bed and dragged ourselves to Mass. Onward, Christian soldiers.

We needed to attend this particular Mass because my parish's Social Justice Committee, which I joined in mid-June, has finally given me a concrete responsibility: hawking raffle tickets for a chance to win one of Father's paintings. All proceeds go to benefit our sister parish in Haiti. Our priest's artwork is Celtic in inspiration—spiral and surreal and trendy but still rather well done. We've set the paintings up on three easels in our high-ceilinged, green-carpeted, very 1990s narthex. By design, the paintings are visible from both exits and even obstruct one. The parishioner who chairs the Social Justice Committee is passionate about the plight of the Haitians and wants no one to be able to escape easily.

I felt rather awkward as I stood between the paintings, trying to project my voice and to stop people as they were fleeing Mass. "Raffle tickets for Haiti. Win Father's artwork," I uttered over and over again with increasing self-consciousness. I felt like a third-rate carnival barker. A bitter old man ran past, his head ducked low in a desperate attempt to evade my gaze. I found myself envying him and hoping that someday I'll be a bitter old Catholic man avoiding people like me.

But though only a handful of people were present—many assumed that the power outages meant no church—we sold a surprising number of tickets, and the experience was good for me. It's good to do something (to help the Church, to help the poor, to help the world), to take some kind of action instead of just thinking about the grand things one might do—while actually doing nothing. And if what I can do is something I can't particularly brag about and that is rather silly, that's just as well. If I'm not willing to embarrass myself in this small way to serve the gospel, what did I learn on Corpus Christi?

Today's epistle reading (2 Cor 8:7, 9, 13–15) strikes exactly this note: "Though he [Jesus] was rich, for your sake he became poor, so that by his poverty you might become rich" (9). If you want to follow the self-emptying Christ, you cannot stand on your dignity.

So—you wanna buy a raffle ticket?

Wednesday of the Thirteenth Week in Ordinary Time

Today is the Fourth of July. Power now restored to our house, we took Beatrice to her first parade, a small one in the incredibly tiny town of Concord, Virginia. There was a train-engine float made by a local church, an airplane float made by another (with "Soldiers in the Army of the Lord" written on it), and a Constitution float (my favorite) made by yet another. On this float, a bunch of teenage boys topped with absurd attempts at white wigs simply sat at old-fashioned school desks. The float's speaker boomed out the Patrick Henry "Liberty or Death" speech, and the wiry, dark-haired kid standing at the podium, obviously aware he was in a ludicrous position, exaggerated his lip sync-ing: each time Patrick Henry made a point, he wagged his chin with comically excessive gravity and raised a knowing eyebrow toward the crowd. There were also fire trucks and a classic car display. Beatrice had a great time, walking back and forth on the sidewalk pretending she was march-ing, frantically waving a little flag handed to her by a Boy Scout, snatching up candy thrown on the street, counting balloons, waving at cars, shaking her fist at any cars that failed to wave back, and even seeing a pony (which was only of moderate interest; fire trucks are way cooler).

I love events like this: what is on parade is school, church, volunteerism, the fabric of small-town America. What is celebrated is as much Concord as the United States. One might even go further. The marchers are asserting that—in spite of all evidence that might suggest the contrary—America is Concord, and Concord is America.

The Prayer after Communion for Independence Day (United States) runs:

> May the love we share in this Eucharist, heavenly
>   Father,
> flow in rich blessing throughout our land
> and by your grace may we as a nation
> place our trust in you and seek to do your will.

The liturgy is quite rightly affirming of patriotism (we want our nation to be richly blessed). But it has its metaphysics right. The things that matter in life are not ultimately derived from any political entity. All that is good in our common life comes from our communion with God and with each other—most literally in the Eucharist—and our nation, any nation, is worth celebrating to the degree that it makes this Eucharistic fellowship possible. It also follows that our nation, any nation, must be fixed to the degree that it is impeding this fellowship.

Our hope is that as a nation we will "place our trust" in God and "seek to do [his] will". Our consolation if that hope fails is that, as G. K. Chesterton points out in a late essay,[3] the foundations of community life preexist all particular political expressions and will survive them. America is valuable insofar as it is like Concord, and Concord may outlive America.

---

[3] See G. K. Chesterton, *The Collected Works of G. K. Chesterton, Vol. 36: The Illustrated London News, 1932–1934*, eds. Lawrence Clipper et. al. (San Francisco: Ignatius Press, 2011), 292.

Tuesday of the Fourteenth Week in Ordinary Time
(Ps 115:3–4, 5–6, 7ab–8, 9–10)

The old dictum runs, "Lex orandi, lex credendi." The law of prayer is the law of belief; as we pray, so will we believe. It's not surprising, then, that throughout Church history people have fought bitterly about the contents of the liturgy; the slightest change alters the world we as believers inhabit.

Take today's Responsorial Psalm (Ps 115:3–4, 5–6, 7ab–8, 9–10) as a case in point. In my Protestant youth, Psalm 115:3 was rendered thus: "Our God is in heaven. He does whatever he wants."[4] In this translation, the verse rightly depicts God as powerful and sovereign but also unintentionally depicts him as capricious, despotic, and arbitrary. Here, God's actions, whether of mercy or judgment, seem to be unbounded by any standard of ethics or rationality. How will God treat you? He'll do whatever he wants.

And as we prayed, so we believed. In our Pentecostal churches, I was raised in a largely irrational universe; we had a healthy respect for God's power and believed fervently in miracles. But for us, miracles were not violations of an otherwise rational, cause-and-effect world order; they were beneficent irrational occurrences in a generally malevolent irrational world. I grew up among people who quite literally attributed a chest cold or a squeaky sofa to demonic possession. (Once you've seen a person try to cast a demon out of a couch, you never forget it.)

But note the difference that an inversion of syntax makes. The verse in our liturgy runs, "Our God is in heaven; / whatever he wills, he does." The emphasis now falls on the idea that there can be no real impediments

---

[4] God's Word Translation.

to the performance of the will of God. The stress falls not on the unknowable character of divine volition but simply on the fact that, for God (unlike for us), there is no real difference between aspiration and action. I can intend to do something and fail to do it—in fact, this is often the case, as my wife has frequently noted. I might put the task off, find the job logistically impossible, or determine that the effort is beyond my means. For God, however, willing and acting are not separate; God need not will in a contingent manner.

This verse presents us with a rational universe, in which there is nothing that can prevent the will of a kind and rational God from being fulfilled. This is a true alternative to the world of idols, believed in by the ancients (and mocked in the rest of Psalm 115), an irrational world where competing and unrelated forces contended for mastery. I don't know if I've fully internalized the Catholic vision of the world even yet, but I do see its beauty. As I pray, I hope someday fully to believe.

Thursday of the Fourteenth Week in Ordinary Time (Hos 11:1–4)

Today we read Hosea 11:1–4:

> When Israel was a child, I loved him,
> out of Egypt I called my son.
> The more I called them,
> the farther they went from me,
> Sacrificing to the Baals
> and burning incense to idols.
> Yet it was I who taught Ephraim to walk....
>
> . . . .

> I fostered them like one
> who raises an infant to his cheeks;
> Yet, though I stooped to feed my child,
> they did not know that I was their healer.

This is a searing image of God's love and Israel's ingratitude, but I wonder if I really understood it until recently. Previously I caught the caustic, aggravated tone of the verse and saw no compassion. How could the Israelites really not know who healed them? Surely they were just seeking an excuse to evade God. Hosea told me a cautionary story of a people callous toward God, but not one with which I could easily identify or from which I could learn.

But now I have a daughter. And I discover for the first time that children have to be taught *everything*. At first, Beatrice didn't even know how to eat. The nurse at the hospital had to sprinkle a little formula on her mouth and on my wife's chest, so she could get the concept; not even that was instinctual. She also didn't initially know how to pee. The nurse again sprinkled a little water on her genitals and got her going, right about the time that the doctors were beginning to wonder if her kidneys were defective. And that was just day one of her life.

Later, we also spent a long time helping her to learn to walk—an operation with which she was unusually slow—helping her to grab furniture, holding her arms in the air above her head, and walking alongside and above her. The list goes on and on. Everything has been learned, and very little of the process is remembered. She doesn't remember that we taught her to walk, since our efforts are recorded in none of the books of photographs about her life that she looks at from time to time and that serve in place of memory. And naturally, there is no photographic record of her learning to nurse or pee that first day in the hospital (we're not *that* kind of family; we have no reality show aspirations). She remembers none of the process; what she has learned has simply become who she is: a little girl who knows how to eat, pee, and walk (all now basically by herself) and who is a disconcertingly close talker, craning her neck and jutting her head within inches of your lips whenever she has something to say to you. And we love her for that.

God loves Israel, and in most respects even what Israel has become. Israel has misattributed the cause of its health and the reason that it has come to maturity, for Israel, like all children, overestimates its reasoning powers and its own maturity. If there is one thing I have learned in recent years, it's that virtually no phenomenon possesses a transparent, indisputable cause. Depending on whom you talk to, the high incidence of psychological disturbance among women who have had an abortion is either because abortion is inherently psychologically damaging or because society excessively stigmatizes abortion. The increasingly high teen pregnancy rate is due either to excessive sex education in schools or insufficient sex education in schools. Nothing, apparently, is transparent, even when it should be. So it's not very surprising that Israel can't remember where it comes from and gets the causal chain wrong.

But events do have causes. God *did* cause Israel to grow and mature, and Israel, having misattributed and forgotten the source of its blessings, will begin to malform itself. I wonder how often this is my story as well. Do I really remember how I came to be who I am, and the myriad moments of grace—some of which I was aware of at the time, some of which I wasn't—that allowed it to happen? Or do I simply assume as a given the life I now possess, as if I just now dropped from the sky fully formed, and yearn for a better self and an easier life? This is the matter of Ordinary Time; this is the hard art of remembering that we as the Church perform collectively by the liturgical calendar.

6

IN THE MIDDLE OF MY LIFE'S WAY
(Ordinary Time, Round 2, Part 2)

Monday of the Fifteenth Week in Ordinary Time (Mt 10:34–11:1)

Many people, including Pope [Emeritus] Benedict XVI in his book *Jesus of Nazareth: From the Baptism in the Jordan to the Transfiguration*, have found the contents of today's Gospel reading (Mt 10:34–11:1) to comprise one of Jesus' more daring pronouncements:

> I have come to set a man against his father, a daughter against her mother, and a daughter-in-law against her mother-in-law; and one's enemies will be those of his household. Whoever loves father or mother more than me is not worthy of me, and whoever loves son or daughter more than me is not worthy of me. (10:35–36)

In short, Jesus divides families and must be preferred over our families.

Judaism is emphatically a religion of descent, a religion of blood, a religion where ties of family and of faith are quite deliberately synonymous. A chosen people. Jesus challenges all that: allegiance to him is what constitutes the true family, even if this allegiance splits the biological family. In a Jewish context, this is radical stuff.

147

But how should we approach this reading in twenty-first-century America, where the idea of splitting the family isn't so radical? Truth be told, we more or less assume as a matter of course that families *will* be split—by divorce, by geography, by self-interest, by difference of opinion. Every family, it seems, contains someone who isn't speaking to someone else and a branch that has simply fallen out of touch with all the others. "A man will be turned against his father," Jesus says. "Of course. Who cares? That's what it means to grow up. We've all got to get on with our lives, right?" we reply. The scandal and offense have largely gone out of the statement.

Maybe what this verse offers us now is some hope for legitimate community. Jesus says that if we are truly to relate to each other as a Church, we may have to allow all our other relationships to break down. Well, in modern America all other forms of relationship have already broken down; there is perhaps nothing the Gospel has to dismantle. Since there is no foundation now, nothing has to be dug up to build anew.

Case in point: A church program paired local college students with families who could give them meals and otherwise watch out for their well-being. My wife and I took on an elementary education major, a student with wild curly red hair and a quiet, self-deprecating sense of humor, a Cincinnati native with a love—found only in that city—for chili served over spaghetti and for the tiny, greasy hamburgers affectionately known as "sliders". Her parents had been divorced almost as long as she could remember. Her father's interest in her life was sporadic. Her mother had spent her life in a series of dead-end waitressing jobs, always looking for the next live-in boyfriend who would make everything right and give life meaning. We helped keep her in school by paying for her car repairs, assisting

with textbooks, handling graduation fees, and having endless conversations, sometimes over that gourmet favorite
Slider Manicotti.[1] As her graduation approached, she told
us that we had done more to help her graduate than had
her real parents. The Church was her family, as Jesus said
it should be. But there wasn't much competition. The
Church may now be virtually our only hope for meaningful connection at all.

Tuesday of the Sixteenth Week in Ordinary Time
(Mt 12:46–50)

In the Gospel today (Mt 12:46–50), Jesus again makes
the radical claim that the Church comprises a truer and
more legitimate form of relationship than that offered by
the biological family. Jesus' true family is simply "whoever does the will of [his] heavenly Father"; these are his
"brother and sister, and mother" and, by implication, ours
as well (50).

This is an inspiring ideal, but one difficult to carry out in
practice. When I was a teenager, a kid whom I hated but
who also attended my family's Pentecostal church unexpectedly moved into my school district. He had dead-
straight greasy brown hair brushed forward and angled
across his forehead. He was always flashing his moped
license, trying (without much success) to attract girls by
convincing them that he could drive. He didn't look
sixteen—he didn't even look his actual fourteen—and the
license indicated in large letters that it applied to mopeds
alone. Since he didn't know anyone in the school, he

---

[1] There is a whole subculture based around using sliders not just as sandwiches but as cooking ingredients.

started sitting next to me every day at lunch, and I endured the mockery of my friends about my new sidekick.

I couldn't stand the derision and after a few weeks told him, "We're not friends at church, and we're not friends here." That was twenty-five years ago, and we have not spoken since. What I said was true, but it reveals the degree to which we were not family, the degree to which the unity in Christ we proclaimed on Sunday was merely a pious pretense. In this moment, I explicitly rejected the gospel.

But it's a lot easier to point out my failings than it is to determine how to live as the family of God. As Thomas à Kempis observes in *The Imitation of Christ*, one way we grow in holiness is simply by tolerating those around us. That's not all family means, but it's one thing family *must* mean. Since the family is not a voluntary association, you put up with your annoying uncle. My cousins and I used to skulk around and glare at each other—even threaten each other—at family gatherings. We deeply resented each other's company, but it never occurred to us that we had any choice but to hang out together.

How can I act like a member of the family of God? Tolerating the people at my parish—even the volunteer musicians whose taste in sacred music differs vastly from my own—would be a real start.

Seventeenth Sunday in Ordinary Time (Jn 6:1–15)

Today's Gospel—and today's homily—focuses on the miracle of the loaves and fishes (Jn 6:1–15). Jesus takes five loaves of bread and two fish from a small boy and feeds five thousand people. Our priest's homily focused on the character of the little boy. He was giving Jesus all he had, and he had no means of getting any more. He was giving up the little he couldn't spare, and couldn't rightly be expected to spare. Who takes away a kid's lunch? But the act of faith—the act of giving away—must be performed without knowing if you will get anything back.

I began—and presently continue—this year of liturgical ruminations not knowing where I will end. Becoming a liturgical subject means giving up your sense of control, your belief that you know what you need—in short, your cherished concept of yourself—and giving it up to Jesus, who gives it back to you transformed.

Some of the harder times for me over the course of this year have been when I have found my concept of myself threatened. What happens to me if my wife persuades me to move uptown and, for the first time in my life, I have to live among rich people? What kind of a college professor have I become if I actually spend more time on accreditation paperwork than on teaching?

As Emily and I discussed over coffee on our screen porch after Mass, we find our fears strangely hard to give up; because our fears are part of who we are, we surrender them with a surprising reluctance. Sigmund Freud argues that fear paradoxically gives you a sense of control over the world: when something terrible happens, you can say you knew it was coming. The world may collapse around you, but your sense of self remains intact; you can even pat yourself on the back for your foresight. Since I am approaching my fortieth birthday, and by the time my parents were forty their marriage was a disaster, I catch myself looking for signs that my own marriage is in trouble. I find no evidence, but still I persist; I want the sense of control that fear brings; if trouble does come, I want to be able to say that I knew it was coming. In some sense, my fears *are* me.

But, of course, part of the point of faith is that my self is not to be defined by me. And how well do I understand myself and my motivation, anyway? As the Psalmist says, my heart is revealed to me only through God, who truly knows it. To be shaped by the liturgy is to end up somewhere different from where you began. This is what it means to be a liturgical subject: to find, in a million different ways, Christ's story becoming your own.

My wife and I are becoming different people over this liturgical year. Today, as Emily stared past the screen porch to the neighbor kids playing across the street, she asked me, "How's this for a plan gone wrong? What if a big house just shows the world how many poor people I could have helped but didn't?" And at Mass, I found myself thinking that if another child is born, we'll find a way to manage.

Most commentators consider the loaves and the fishes to be a Eucharistic miracle. Perhaps it comes down to this: every week Jesus takes what we think we cannot spare and transfigures it to be shared with the community, so that we too may in our own smaller miracles be given over to others.

Wednesday of the Seventeenth Week in Ordinary Time (Jer 15:10, 16–21)

Jeremiah's prophetic call, related in the first reading for today (Jer 15:10, 16–21), begins the way we might expect. He eats the words of God, and they become his "joy" and "the happiness of [his] heart" (16). They give his life purpose, meaning, and direction and make it worthwhile. They do what we expect faith to do.

But sometimes your life is easier if it lacks purpose or meaning. Precisely because of the divine word he bears, Jeremiah is alienated (he sits "alone"); he is a problem for his family, and an object of scorn, "curse[d]" by everyone (17, 10). He is "a man of strife and contention to all the land" (10). He is simply miserable and suffers as if he has an "incurable" wound (18). He is doomed to tell everyone what no one wants to hear. Surely, his life would have been easier and more pleasant if he could just have worked a job, done what was expected of him, tried his best to get along with everyone, kept his opinions to himself—or tried prudently not to have opinions—then clocked out and had a beer at the end of the day.

Over the past few weeks, I've been reflecting on the blessings that come with belonging to the community of faith, but one pays a price as well; particularly, a person who fully embraces the community of faith is often excluded from other communities. Hilaire Belloc, the great Edwardian Catholic man of letters, counts up these costs in his masterwork, *The Path to Rome*. Belloc, who had a gift for friendship and was the life of every party, felt keenly that in the modern world the way of faith is the way of alienation. He writes:

> I know that we who return [to the Faith] suffer hard things; for there grows a gulf between us and our contemporaries. We are perpetually thrust into minorities, and the world almost begins to talk a strange language....
>
> And this is hard: that the Faith begins to make one abandon the old way of judging.... The very nature of social force seems changed to us. And this is very hard when a man has loved common views and is happy only with his fellows....
>
> But the hardest thing of all is that it leads us away, as by a command, from all the banquet of the intellect than which there is no keener joy known to man.
>
> I went slowly up the village place in the dusk, thinking of this deplorable weakness in men that the Faith is too great for them, and accepting it as an inevitable burden. I continued to muse with my eyes upon the ground....

> By the Lord! I begin to think this intimate religion as
> tragic as a great love.... Yes, certainly religion is as tragic
> as first love, and drags us out into the world and away from
> our dear homes.

I too would be more at ease, both professionally and
personally, among my coworkers and college friends if
I could just share the agnostic progressivism that forms
their common vocabulary and common culture. I have
lost friends once they realized that I actually meant what I
said when I professed the Faith, that I wasn't a "thinking
Catholic" or a "progressive Catholic" but simply a Catholic. One time this was done by a note slipped under my
apartment door by a former friend who never spoke to me
again. The note said, "People whose philosophies are as
different as ours cannot remain friends."

So what is gained by following God? From an eternal
perspective, of course, the beatific vision, life with God
himself. More immediately, God promises in the latter
part of the Jeremiah reading to make the prophet "a solid
wall of brass" against the people (15:20); he will not be
swayed by them, but he may sway some of them. In faith,
Jeremiah becomes an individual. His identity is as solid
as brass. And what individual was more unique, flamboyant, and entertaining than Hilaire Belloc? By being cut off,
both Belloc and Jeremiah were saved from being merely
faces in the crowd. They were rooted in the eternal, so
when alone, cut off and alienated, they could still stand.

Thursday of the Seventeenth Week in Ordinary Time
(Jer 18:1–6)

Writing these reflections sometimes gets laborious. Sometimes it seems forced and false. I know that a writing

prompt awaits me when I wake up in the morning, and I have to make a deadline by the end of the day. At times, I feel like I'm summarizing whatever events I have encountered in my day, and then trying to jam the Scripture readings on them one way or the other. In such moments, writing these reflections almost seems more like a loss of meaning than a gain. To go back to my reflections yesterday, it's not so troublesome to live a life that appears to lack an apparent meaning or pattern if you weren't looking for one in the first place. The person who simply lives an animal existence untroubled by matters of the spirit lives a reduced life but not always an unpleasant one.

This seems hardest in Ordinary Time. It is a long grind, without obvious narrative arc and pattern. The grand events of Christ's life, the dramatic moments in the Church calendar, are either before or after this liturgical season. Ordinary Time is an in-between time, when Pentecost is over and Advent has not yet begun. Since Advent refers in part to the Second Coming of Christ, the Church has been living in Ordinary Time since the first Pentecost. Ordinary Time is our time.

So how do we live between times? In part by looking to the Church. The Holy Spirit has entered the Church, and we can see that there is meaning, that God has entered the world, through the work of the Church. No other organization in human history has been truly worldwide. No other group of people has pledged itself from the first to helping the poorest of the poor. Most of the good aspects of the modern world were originally created by the Church—universities, hospitals, orphanages, mass education. Despite all her faults, the Church is the primary tangible evidence that the world is not simply a Darwinian struggle. The Church is the main sign Christ has left us to assure us that the world still has meaning. There was an Incarnation. Existence is not without a key.

We see just enough meaning to discern that there *is* a pattern. But we live between times and can't quite make it out. Only after the end of time is the full pattern of time visible and complete. The Jeremiah reading for today (18:1–6) gets at this. God is the potter, and we are the clay (6); he is making us and the world as he sees fit. But what can the clay perceive of this process? It can see that alteration is happening, surely, but it cannot see the process' direction and final end. This is where we live in Ordinary Time.

Transfiguration of Our Lord (Mk 9:2–10)

But at moments the pattern breaks through. Yesterday we met some friends for lunch in Charlottesville, Virginia, a town best known as the home of the University of Virginia. I've known the wife in the couple for over twenty years, since we were both teens in Detroit-area Pentecostal churches. She has been, in turns, a starving nanny, a Christian recording artist (on a respectable label, with tours and such), an entry-level art museum curator, a starving nanny again, and a high school teacher; now she is a stay-at-home mom. She can live basically anywhere and deal with basically anything. She'll weep, she'll laugh, she'll move on. I don't know whether to attribute her resilience to her faith or to her being a Detroiter. Probably both.

Like everyone else from Michigan, she long ago left the state to find work; she now lives in the D.C. suburbs, only a few hours from me. Together we were intense, moody, "alternative" teens who doubted whether we would ever find adult work; together we finally got professional jobs (we started the same month); together we found ourselves entering marriage and parenthood more or less late in life, after we had both figured we would spend our lives single. Now we watch Beatrice playing with my friend's daughter at a hamburger joint on Charlottesville's very college-town pedestrian mall.

Ellie's parents have disappeared to the bathroom, since infant sister Olivia's diaper has exploded all over their clothes. Emily and I can't fully control both Beatrice and Ellie, and the restaurant is mostly empty. So Beatrice and Ellie run around a supporting pole. They "clean" the restaurant's subway tile with napkins, they dance, they spin in circles until they fall down, they jump up and dramatically hug, and then they giggle. For a moment, the adults in the room don't exist, the restaurant doesn't exist, just these two little girls working out their relationship with each other and with the world.

Our two-year-old daughter has never played with another child like this before. And it's with the ketchup-devouring, wild-haired child of my old friend. I'm witnessing a flash-forward in time to my daughter's teen years, or a flashback in time to my own. These children are immortal souls, and there are moments when this fact shines forth and they seem older and wiser than their age allows, as if the spirit is about to burst the body's limitations.

Today is the Feast of the Transfiguration. I know my daughter isn't the Christ and isn't transfigured. I assert only the dimmest of analogies. But this is what it means to be the *imago Dei*: we're a dim analogy for God. In today's Gospel reading (Mk 9:2–10), the disciples are witnessing a break in time, the glory of the post-Resurrection Christ shining forth prematurely, the Christ of the Second Coming, the Christ of the apocalypse manifesting during his earthly life and ministry. Then it is gone. Their sight—and possibly Jesus' mortal body—can handle only so much.

Saturday of the Eighteenth Week in Ordinary Time
(Hab 1:12–2:4)

In today's first reading (Hab 1:12–2:4), the Hebrew prophet Habakkuk tries to give us perspective on the confusions and trials of life. He tells us that if the world we see before us does not align with God's will or promises, then we just haven't waited long enough. "The vision still has its time, presses on to fulfillment, and will not disappoint. If it delays, wait for it, it will surely come, it will not be late" (2:3).

I was raised a Pentecostal, a member of a faith tradition that expects more or less daily displays of the miraculous. By early high school, I was slipping into agnosticism, partly because I was maddened by the line of thinking Habakkuk represents. To me, the injunction to wait on God sounded like simple psychological denial, a refusal in the face of all the evidence to accept that reality didn't bear your wishes out. It smacked of saying, "Someday my prince will come," when you're actually (as I would have pointed out) waiting for Godot.

I realize now that Habakkuk is making a statement about the nature of time. God's times and seasons are not our own. If we expect the world to run according to our timetable, we don't truly believe that God is the ultimate reality. We're holding our quantifiable world to be the real world, the frame into which God is supposed to fit. Habakkuk's refusal of our normal conception of time is not the evasion I once took it to be; it's a metaphysical challenge.

It's hard to alter how we conceive of time, how we think of the lives we inhabit. God's time invades and threatens our time in several different ways. Sometimes, as in Habakkuk, God breaks our concept of time by

delay. We think we know the right time for divine intervention, the moment when God must act or all will be
lost. But, as in the raising of Lazarus or the Resurrection of Jesus, divine time sometimes means waiting to
act until, as far as we're concerned, all *is* lost. If Jesus
had hurried on to heal Lazarus before he had died or had
proactively evaded the Romans and avoided the crucifixion, the coming of the Kingdom would actually have
been delayed. The divine irruption into time would
have been muted or put off.

At other times, divine time means—as in the case of
Saint Paul the apostle or Saint Francis of Assisi—that God
commands and moves too quickly, demanding action right
now, before anything is put in order. Shouldn't there have
been a longer delay between Saint Paul killing Christians
and leading them as an apostle? Or between Saint Francis experiencing an internal conversion and founding a
religious order meant to reform the whole Church and
world? I would think so; I'm always scandalized by God's
haste when I read the accounts of the ministries of Paul
and Francis.

Finally, divine time can mean learning to read the
divine seasons in which our lives and world actually move,
which are contiguous with but not identical to those of
our workweek or the solar calendar. Jesus taught Nicodemus about the seasons of the world. And in the third
chapter of Ecclesiastes, we learn about reading the patterns
in our lives that we could easily miss, the times for every
purpose under heaven.

The liturgical year is the most concrete manifestation
of divine time we have, and it can disrupt our concepts of
time in all three ways. Throughout this year, I have been
trying to learn from the liturgy to read the patterns of my

life. And to wait. And to be ready. I hope I'm getting somewhere.

As I write, Emily and I begin waiting to see if we will have a second child. Last night, we sat up in bed and finally reached a concrete resolution:

EMILY: Okay, so we're open to a second child now. Genesis 1:28: "Be fruitful and multiply." I get it. I agree with it. But I hate the pressure.

CHENE: Pressure?

EMILY: The pressure to make it work. It's been a few years since Beatrice was born. I might not be able to pull it off anymore. I might be a cracked cistern.

CHENE: I'm older than you are. I might be a dry reed.

EMILY: Doesn't matter. When it comes to infertility, everyone always blames the woman. I've got friends in their midthirties who've spent thousands of dollars trying to conceive. And all they've got for it is self-hate. You know me. You know I can't stand it when I can't make something work.

CHENE: Do we have to *make* anything work? I don't want to sound too simplistic, but is this whole thing really up to us, anyway?

EMILY: Well, really, no. In the end, it's up to God. I guess I could just throw away my folder full of Natural Family Planning charts and try not to worry about it.

CHENE: And then we'll sail off into uncharted waters and see what happens.

So we sail off into uncharted waters, wondering if we have the time and purpose right.

Assumption of the Blessed Virgin Mary (August 15)
(1 Cor 15:54b–57)

This year, the Feast of the Assumption coincides with the opening of the academic year. Summer over, I'm back to leading my so-called Accreditation Task Force, back to the life-consuming project I only sort of understand and for which I've only sort of been given any kind of support or backup.

We had a four-hour accreditation meeting this morning. We were each required to bring our university-issued iPad, the purpose of which I've never discovered, since the iPad is incapable of running any of the software needed for the type of work we are doing. We were herded with our iPads into a library conference room that positively radiated with fluorescent light. We were seated at a bunch of long tables and stuffed with weak coffee and mini muffins. Then the lights went out, and we endured computer-enhanced presentation after computer-enhanced presentation, each containing colorful pictures, nice graphics, and neat special effects (who knew that words could spin in circles and then bounce off the page like that?). The color-coded pie charts and line graphs were especially pretty, and especially frequent. Institutions like complicated charts. Charts are shiny. Charts are colorful. Charts look professional. Charts produce an illusory sense that everything is organized and under control. But it soon became increasingly clear that, for all the nice formatting and all the pretty pictures, we were going to hear nothing that practically clarified what our job was and how we would do it.

So after the second or third presentation, everyone stopped listening. A humanities professor who is quick with a smile, quick with a joke, and always impeccably dressed—obviously the popular girl in high school and a prominent figure on campus now—began passing snarky notes around the room. Then everyone started using the university wireless to e-mail snide comments to each other on the iPads, marking the first time we had ever used these devices for any meaningful purpose. I imagine that a four-hour meeting is equally unproductive in any office. The tedium brings out the juvenile in everyone. We left the meeting more convinced than ever that we have no idea what we're doing or how we're going to handle this job.

We also left with hard-copy printouts of Tom's Planner calendars (if you don't know what they are, don't worry; I didn't either). They are electronic scheduling calendars with interlocking schedules of due dates, color-coded blue, green, purple, yellow, and red; put it all together, and you get as many possible combinations as on a Rubik's Cube. Blue represents first draft; orange, second draft; purple, third draft; and red, supporting documents, on twenty-five accreditation standards, all dancing in and out in intricate patterns that dominate the next year of my life. I can barely follow the calendar, let alone envision how I will live it. I feel like I've been swallowed up by a computerized presentation and will be living in a wonderland of line graphs.

The Tom's calendar reminds me strangely of the liturgical year, with its interlocking cycles of variable feasts and fixed feasts; years A, B, and C; and symbolic color coding. But the process and effects of the Tom's calendar are the reverse of those of the liturgical calendar. The Tom's calendar breaks my life into pieces and quantifies it, removing any sense that my life has a holistic meaning. The Christian philosopher Søren Kierkegaard said, "Purity of the heart is to will one thing." The idea that one could will *one* thing or orient one's attention in any single direction lies outside this timetable's conceptual categories. The liturgical calendar, by contrast, takes the quantifiable minutiae of my life and works them into meaningful patterns, through its very complexity restoring wholeness to what was split and divided.

Mary was immaculately conceived and finally—at the last instant of her earthly life, or perhaps even after her death (the Church has left the point open)—assumed into heaven. Holiness can begin with the conception of life itself and continue to the final moment of terrestrial existence. Mary's body—not just her soul, but the whole of her being—was taken into heaven; in Paul's words recited today (1 Cor 15:54b–57, second reading), "that which is mortal clothe[d] itself with immortality" (54). It's a goal to aspire to—that the totality of one's life would be worthy of being received into God, that the whole of one's existence would be divinely ratified. There can be a single pattern. It *is* possible to will one thing.

How can I live a life that actually aspires to heaven, that matches the patterns of the stars, that moves to the pageant of the liturgical rather than the Tom's calendar? One could do worse than following the example of the Queen of Heaven.

Twentieth Sunday in Ordinary Time (Prov 9:1–6)

Sticking with the trope of wise women, today's first reading (Prov 9:1–6) gives us one of the most famous moments in Proverbs. Wisdom (personified as a woman—Lady Wisdom) builds a house (1). The point is clear: wisdom is the origin of everything that lasts and stands. My wife has been obsessed all year with either building a new house or renovating an old one. My wife is wise and even has the papers to prove it: a Ph.D. from a major university. For the last year, I have been living this metaphor; I've been watching a wise woman prepare to build a house.

And perhaps now I understand this metaphor better. Proverbs contrasts the voice of Lady Wisdom with the voice of Lady Folly and depicts the soul as caught between these voices, which continually summon all of us as we walk the streets and go about our lives. Folly is more appealing than Wisdom in part because Folly speaks in broad strokes and grand gestures and convenient oversimplifications. Folly tells us what we want to hear. The voice of Wisdom is the voice of prudence, the voice of precision. As a home builder, Wisdom is a craftsman. You can really trust only the person who knows and understands the precise details of the job to make important decisions that create or shape the structures of your life, the house in which you live.

But the details are so excruciatingly boring. The thousands of hours my wife has spent researching home building and remodeling are incomprehensible to me. And I never know when she'll ambush me with a barrage of information. I'll think I'm sitting safely at dinner, and then out of nowhere she'll begin to explain five different ways to blow out a wall, each of which would have a different effect on architecture and decor. She loses me at step one: I'm still thinking, we have to blow out a wall? Doesn't that happen only in action movies? Won't we all die?

We'll be pulling out of the driveway on the way to church and I'll be checking the rearview mirror to make sure Beatrice is safely installed in the car seat, and Emily will start explaining seven different approaches we might take toward appliances. I can conceive of the difference between none of them, though I do get distracted enough to miss the traffic light.

We'll be upstairs checking e-mail at the end of the day, with sleep blissfully in sight, and without warning she'll pull out the drafting paper and start drawing a potential addition. She has done this so many times that I have no idea which version of the plan we're talking about anymore:

"What do you think of supporting columns that double as bookcases?"

"What about kitchen cabinets in the family room?"

"What about an under-the-sink dishwasher?"

"What about an eight-foot bump-out in the TV room, turning it into an office that could double as a bedroom, and putting a sleeping nook in the window?"

I tune out, although every idea of hers for decorating or altering that we've ever tried has worked out well. I can't stand the details. I would rather just hire a dishonest contractor who will paint a picture in broad strokes and tell me a lot of happy lies than have to listen to my wife's continuing research.

We may relate to the Church in a similar manner. The Church's teaching about morality and human nature is so subtle and so nuanced, full of exceptions and qualifiers and conditions and detailed case studies, that people often reject it. The mind accustomed to think in the 140 characters of Twitter finds the nuances of Catholicism an obfuscation and an evasion. "Give me the Simple Gospel, not these myriad technicalities," we complain. One famous analogy—I think it is Chesterton's, though I cannot find the passage—is that if a man tells you never to drink alcohol, then he is just a moralizing teetotaler and can be easily ignored. But if he tells you to avoid a particular pub at a particular intersection, and you go there anyway and are beaten and robbed, then you have reason to believe him. Wisdom means understanding the particulars of humanity.

The voice of Folly too cries in the street, and it's easy to see why it sounds better. But what kind of a world would Twitter build? I fear that we may soon find out.

Thursday of the Twentieth Week in Ordinary Time
(Mt 22:1–14)

Jesus tells us today that God's Kingdom is essentially a banquet or a party (Mt 22:1–14, today's Gospel). A truly good party—of which there are few—is really a consummation of the human experience. No one I know throws a better party than my friend who is a poet now teaching at a small Catholic college near Chicago. The product of a military family, he adapted to being carted continually from place to place by developing a personality that could get conversation out of a wall, and an imagination that imposes itself upon circumstances. In graduate school, he threw a 1940s theme party—formal dress required, big band music on the CD player, elaborate retro cocktails— where dance majors levitated across the floor while poets spoke of the good things of our common life and of God. At another party (which he didn't host), he enforced leisure; he brought a Wiffle-ball bat and whacked anyone who spoke of work. Only he could make pretentious graduate students stop their chatter and carve jack-o'-lanterns while drinking cheap beer. My friend is a festive soul, and he more or less compelled my often-reclusive self to come into his fellowship. A good party is music, comradeship, breaking of bread, elemental connection. It truly is like the Kingdom of heaven.

And God understands us well enough to know that, like the guests invited to the wedding feast in Jesus' parable, we're too stupid to want to come. Our desires are ill formed. We're tired, we're lazy, we're slothful—I actually had to dress as Sloth for another of his theme parties, which was conceptually difficult—and we prefer (as C. S. Lewis notes in *The Great Divorce*) to be left alone. So God in his mercy compels us to come to his party. He has taken our measure, and in his mercy, sometimes it's enough (humanly speaking) if we're just willing to play along and not put up too much resistance.

And this is the wonder of the Church and the sacraments, the whole doctrine of merit. God takes us at more than our word and gives us more than we ask. We can be unworthy beggars; we just have to throw on something that at least looks like party clothes. If we stumble through the motions, half-sincere, full of attrition, devoid of contrition, he treats us like the contrite saint and will—half by transforming ourselves, half in spite of ourselves—bring us to holiness and to his Kingdom.

Twenty-First Sunday in Ordinary Time (Jn 6:60–69)

In today's Gospel (Jn 6:60–69), Peter says that Jesus has "the words of eternal life" (Jn 6:69). If we wish to live, there is no one else to whom we can turn. The priest, in his homily, parsed the Gospel as meaning not that Jesus had words that would take the suffering out of life but that Jesus' teachings make life endurable by giving suffering meaning. All existence inevitably involves suffering.

In *Beyond the Pleasure Principle*, Sigmund Freud quite rightly says that the only way to be free from difficulty, suffering, anxiety, and change is to be dead. We typically live our lives fleeing suffering, but we can't possibly succeed. No one puts the point more clearly than Thomas à Kempis: No matter what choices we make, we cannot evade the cross.[2] Those who join the priesthood or religious life have courageously accepted the cross—giving up their preferences, plans, and self-will—explicitly and at one blow. They know they will live lives of loss and denial for Christ.

God in his mercy allows the rest of us to take our suffering in daily installments that we repackage and relabel to avoid facing what they are. But we too must take up our cross daily if we are to be saved. So we get married, inspired by love and sexual desire, often expecting that our spouse will "complete" us and give us all we need (while we give little in return). And most likely, we end up with children, and a ceaseless round of often-thankless responsibilities—which is actually what we need.

I think frequently of the irony that I opted against the religious life in part because I didn't think I could handle a structured schedule and discipline and I didn't think I could live for others. And now my life looks like this:

5:00	Rise and get ready
5:30	Watch Beatrice while Emily gets ready
6:00	Breakfast
6:15	Take dog out
6:30	Leave for work, listening to the Bible on an audio CD
7:00	Still driving, switch from listening to audio Bible to praying the rosary
7:30	Arrive at work and prepare for class
8:00–2:00	Teach courses and hold office hours
2:00	Leave to pick up Beatrice, listening to a job-related audiobook
3:00	Pick up Beatrice
3:15	Take dog out with Beatrice

[2] See Thomas à Kempis, *Imitation of Christ*, book II, chapter XII.

3:00–5:00	Watch Beatrice while Emily finishes her workday
5:30	Dinner
6:00	Put Beatrice to bed
6:15	Take dog out
6:30–bedtime	Catch up on grading, reading for classes, and student e-mail

Because I have duties to God and others that I must fulfill, my life has gradually become as structured as a Benedictine monk's. This has happened stage by stage, and I would have refused these changes if I had ever realized that the day would come when any time that was simply mine, to do with as I pleased, would shrink to zero. When I was a single man, I regularly went to bed at an hour not long before that at which I now rise. But, really, we're not supposed to live for ourselves, and for the most part I enjoy the rigidly structured life I would never have consciously chosen. God mercifully will not let us escape the cross. We have to die to ourselves and cannot escape the words of everlasting life. God compels us to come into his Kingdom.

Twenty-Second Sunday in Ordinary Time
(Deut 4:1–2, 6–8)

As I teach the early weeks of the academic year, the liturgical year has been featuring a series of readings about the true nature of wisdom. Today's first reading (Deut 4:1–2, 6–8) says that the Mosaic law is Israel's "wisdom and intelligence" (6). This seems counterintuitive. As Americans, we tend to think of wisdom as an individual possession, something that can be measured in a test or registered in a moment of crisis. But here, wisdom is the collective possession of the People of God, the community of faith.

Wisdom is another benefit of entering into the Kingdom, of making the sacrifices necessary to belong to God. So how does this work?

Biblically, wisdom is a way of seeing, a way of understanding the world, a way of existing, a mode of life. Deuteronomy attributes Israel's wisdom to the Mosaic law, which is at first glance surprising but is really utterly reasonable, since a code of law is a systematized representation of a mode of life. For instance, the Declaration of Independence paints an ideal American existence—full of "life, liberty, and the pursuit of happiness"—while the less exciting Constitution tries to pin down concretely how this ideal would work in day-to-day existence.

As many postmodern thinkers (such as Louis Althusser and Michel Foucault) have pointed out, any code of law—whether American civil law, the Mosaic law, or canon law—shapes the identities and perceptions of those subject to it. Laws condition how people perceive themselves and the world around them. For instance, what is a "good American" or a "good Catholic"? Well, at the very least, he is a person who stays within the boundaries set by civil or Church law, whether he likes these particular laws or not. If what we do (and don't do) shapes who we are, we are all creatures of law (even rebels against the law are defined by the law, just by inversion).

Most postmodern thinkers mistakenly see our law-bound condition as a problem (rather than as an inevitable aspect of human nature: we are social creatures who must live in community). But they are basically right about the influence law has on our lives. The laws we live under—even the mere fast before the Eucharist and the Sunday duty—shape our consciousness, become internalized like a reflex. Consequently, the people whose laws reflect God's revelation will be a wise people, even if, like Israel and the early Church, they lack economic prosperity and formal education. Their outlooks have been shaped more wisely than they know.

The traditional Catholic who simply accepts the Faith and neither analyzes nor questions it has gut-level responses to life and the world shaped by the writings of Thomas Aquinas, Augustine of Hippo, John Paul II, Yves Congar, and thousands of other intellectual giants, whose names he has never even heard. Their teachings are embodied in the Catechism, in the Code of Canon Law; he has never read them, but they form his mental universe. The modern skeptic has, by virtue of his skepticism, cut himself off from the whole of accumulated human wisdom, of all cultures and religions. Effectually, he operates off of forty years of accumulated wisdom rather than six thousand. The Catholic traditionalist auto mechanic is, then, as an individual and as a human subject, wiser than the secularist university professor.

In part, this critique applies to me as well. As a convert, I accept the Faith but have not yet fully internalized it. I can argue for it effectively, but nothing about it is instinctual, and many of my steps are false. In spending this year with the liturgy, I'm trying to work out longhand what a faithful Catholic does automatically in his head. In a sense, I'm trying to learn to be an auto mechanic through correspondence classes. I dare to hope that, as at the end of a long set of math homework problems, something is by now starting to click.

Wednesday of the Twenty-Fourth Week in Ordinary Time (1 Cor 12:31–13:13)

The day before I turn forty, the Church asks me to read Saint Paul on putting away childish things, on learning not to talk like a child or reason like a child, on growing up (1 Cor 12:31–13:13, today's epistle).

As fate would have it, I also find myself teaching Dante's *Inferno* in my World Literature classes this week. The most famous of all Catholic poems begins with the poet's assertion that he has become lost "in the middle of his life's way". In middle age, he suddenly realizes that he is no longer on the right path, but he doesn't know exactly when he strayed from the road or how he got to where he is now. A personal inventory, guided by Virgil and Beatrice,[3] now begins that will end in Dante's redemption.

Midlife is a kind of stock taking, precisely because by this point one's life begins to take shape; enough decisions have been made that one's life begins to assume a concrete form beyond the mere guesses, fears, and dreams of youth. I can't begin to wonder if the life I've made is the life I would have wanted until I've made something of a life. But middle age is the time when change is still possible, as life has not yet entirely taken its course; there are reasons why there is typically no "old-life crisis".

I wonder whether, when I read back over this year of ruminations after its completion, I will come to see that a large part of the story has been Emily and I moving into middle age. I will find us taking stock of our lives, torn between the temptations of middle age (such as justifying one's existence by buying a huge house, which was narrowly rejected) and the more salutary spiritual inventory that Dante represents (determining to give more to the Church, to act for social justice, to be open to another child). Certainly, this has been very explicit lately, as we've been up late each of the last several nights hashing through

---

[3] Yes, I must reluctantly admit, my daughter is named after a character in Dante. English teachers do that sort of thing.

the anxieties of midlife. I simply don't know how to feel about a life that is full of blessings I never asked for or deserved and that lacks other goods that I've desired.

So what does it mean to put away childish things rather than fall into a midlife crisis or simply accept "the resignation that living brings", to quote one of my father's more unfortunate heroes, the 1970s pop singer Jackson Browne?[4] Paul's ruminations are about the passage from time to eternity, but they could also extend to a lesser extent to stages of life. Saint Paul tells us that prophecy and knowledge will die, while love will live. Of course, we need divine insight and spiritual knowledge all our lives. But perhaps they are spiritual gifts particularly attuned to the past and future tenses; knowledge refers to what has been and prophecy to what will come to be. Maybe the reason why love is the gift that remains is that it requires no past or future tense; it can exist in the eternal present. Love, as Paul explains it, is directed toward what is, not toward what might be (1 Cor 13:13).

Middle age should be a time of love, of making real the commitments—to the Catholic Church, to my wife—that I have made in faith and hope, though I couldn't fully know what I meant when I made them. I begin to find out whether I really do love, as I leave aside childish things, the future-oriented virtues of youth. I begin to see whether I can handle being fully known by another person—how, I sometimes think, I must bore my wife; how could anyone tolerate my conversation daily for a decade?—and whether I can ultimately handle loving and being loved by God. When I pledge my vows to my wife or to God, I can know only in part what I'm doing and must count on faith

---

[4] The quotation, which I have always hated, is from Browne's song "Before the Deluge".

and hope to make up the rest. But coming to live this out, coming to know and be known, is a very different, and more difficult, matter.

And this involves ceasing to live in the future and putting aside fantasy, coming to live in the real and caring about the daily decisions with which one is confronted. Can I handle what is in front of me? Not insist on my own way? Bear all things? Believe all things? Pick up my cross daily? Or do I have a false faith that actually is a fantasy about a world where none of these virtues will be necessary? To manage this, to move more fully into reality, is a worthy work of midlife.

7

OUT OF FANTASY, INTO ACTUALITY
(Ordinary Time, Round 2, Part 3)

Monday of the Twenty-Fifth Week in Ordinary Time
(Ps 15:2–3a, 3bc–4ab, 5)

I'm easily disturbed or shaken. I always want to imagine
myself as a fearless hero of the Faith, but on my first sacra-
mental confession after turning forty, I listed cowardice as
my dominant recent sin. I desire to dodge or accommodate when I possibly can. Especially at work, I am prone
just to play along, try to keep things running, and draw no
more attention to myself than I have to.

And I am prone to fear. One of the most recent fruits
of this liturgical year has been a joint family decision not
to move into a bigger house but just to make some slight
changes to this house and give the money saved to the
local parish, other worthy religious organizations, and
the poor (we are increasing our level of charitable giving
to 20 percent of our income). But psychologically, I hate
remodeling. I dread the prospect of having furniture piled
up in unlikely places and the house ripped up and patched
together. Even when we just had some work done on
our porch, I heard the sledgehammer smashing concrete
and became convinced that the side wall of the house was
going to cave in. For the rest of the day, I couldn't muster sufficient mental focus even to read. I don't need a

75

psychologist to make sense of my phobia of remodeling. The symbolism is painfully obvious; as the product of a broken home, even in middle age, I can't stand to have my house broken up.

If you want to throw me, you've got a fairly easy job ahead of you. So today's Responsorial Psalm (Ps 15:2–3a, 3bc–4ab, 5), which explains how a person can "never be disturbed" (5), how one can avoid being the Prufrockian creature that I often am, is of particular interest. The Psalm gives a very concrete program for being calm and self-possessed: I must speak the truth (2), avoid slander (3), distrust those who do not fear God (4), honor those who do fear God (4), keep my word when it tells against me (4), and refuse bribes and lend without interest (5). "He who does these things / shall never be disturbed" (5) (or, in some translations, "moved" or "shaken").

Part of the Psalm's teaching is fairly obvious. We could have guessed it, even if we don't always live this way. If you speak the truth, you need not fear being caught out in a falsehood. If you don't slander, you don't have to worry about the revenge of those whom you've slandered. If you don't trust those who are unworthy of trust (and the ungodly generally are), then you won't have the trauma of their betrayal. Knowing whom to trust and avoiding slander are (at least for me) both questions of identity. Most of the times in recent years that I have slandered or spoken ill of others, it has been because that is what passes for conversation at my place of employment. I was trashing others as the culture required rather than taking the Church as my primary community.

But what is most interesting to me in this Psalm is that the righteous person is *not* promised happiness or prosperity. What he is promised is stability, which is more valuable than prosperity or happiness, but which comes at a price. The price of never being moved is that you keep your word even when it's inconvenient and tells against you, that you lend others money without taking the interest you could have made. When you're not out for a personal profit, and you don't fear personal loss, then you will not be moved. You can no longer be manipulated, because you have pulled out of the scheme of rewards and punishments on which a materialistic society operates and have begun to operate only on divine rewards and punishments.

Presently, things are going well financially for my wife and me; among other things, I got a substantial raise last week. We've been able to use the money to do things like save a former student of Emily's from being evicted from her apartment a week before she starts a new job that will allow her to pay her bills (this happened just last Friday). We got the check to the student the day we discussed it, and she received it at four o'clock, just in time to pay by five o'clock and not be evicted. It's wonderful to be able—and willing—to do this. This liturgical year has really changed how we look at the world. But we will be truly stable in our commitments and unmoved only if we are generous in adversity as well as prosperity. That test still lies ahead.

Thursday of the Twenty-Fifth Week in Ordinary Time
(Eccl 1:2–11)

Unsurprisingly, since the liturgical year is always one step ahead of me, the Church now asks me to begin pondering adversity through the skeptical wisdom of Ecclesiastes and Job. The one sort of adversity I already face—and that probably all Christians must face—is alienation. Like many

Americans, I lead a life oriented toward responsibilities to work and family and, regrettably, haven't managed to branch out socially much beyond that. So, for the most part, my coworkers comprise my social circle. My colleagues are in the main nice people who care about their students. We make small talk by complaining about work, as people do at any job, but our complaints are insincere. We're glad to be doing what we're doing. We get along pretty well.

But although our offices might be physically adjacent, metaphysically we inhabit fundamentally different universes. Most of my colleagues are radical postmoderns who believe in neither sin, nor human nature, nor objective truth. These are the operating assumptions through which they understand the world and that they spend their professional lives trying to convey to others.

I don't mean to be melodramatic here. I'm not even sure that public colleges are peculiarly irreligious. My restaurant coworkers weren't much interested in the concepts of sin or objective truth either. They did whatever they wanted—from drug dealing to petty theft—and answered to no external authority or ideal; they just didn't bother to make speeches about it. Probably, your workplace is in its own way as alienating as my own.

Still, I look at my colleagues, who have treated me graciously and whom I generally like, and find myself wondering, "How can I talk to these people about anything that matters—much less ultimate things?" How can any of us convey to postmoderns who believe in neither sin, nor human nature, nor objective truth that it's the truth that Christ renews our sinful nature? This isn't a simple question, and it's hard to find answers that really work. To communicate with anyone, we must first establish some shared assumptions, some initial operating premises that can be granted both ways. Right now, between the

Church and the common culture, these are few, and this makes conversation nearly impossible.

Among people who have children, the latest news about your kids serves as the fallback topic of conversation if you can't think of anything else to say. But some of my coworkers feel that the nuclear family is a fascist structure that holds American society in an oppressive stranglehold; they consider bringing your kids into the conversation to be an act of aggression. "A decent person—if she'd only shut up about her kids" is a moral judgment I've heard proclaimed more than once. And, even if the objection to children as a topic of conversation weren't explicit, it's hard to tell stories about one's children to people who aren't sure that children should exist. As I've mentioned, when I announced our pregnancy to one of my most gregarious departmental colleagues, he responded, "Are you happy about it? Was it planned?" He and I maintain cordial relations, but I've never been able to look at him the same way again, and I haven't brought up anything serious to him since.

Besides family, church occupies most of my thought and my time. The professor who hates organized religion has become a stereotype, and the stereotype is not entirely without foundation. I've accidentally shut down many a friendly lunchtime conversation by mentioning church. Since I openly professed my Catholic faith to the campus in a public talk last August, one formerly chatty professor has now begun to avoid me, and when we must meet he beholds me with a bemused smirk and bugged-out eyes. He clearly now thinks he is talking to a space alien.

So what is left as a conversation topic when faith and family are both off the table? Mostly, there is coffee. My colleagues and I drop in and out of each other's offices for enormously long conversations about gourmet coffee. We discuss such pressing questions as these:

- Are coffee-of-the-month clubs a worthwhile commitment?
- Are coffee-of-the month clubs too mainstream? Are the best coffees those shipped directly from (the perennially cool) New York City or those shipped from (the Southern hipster mecca) Asheville, North Carolina?
- Is regular coffee shipped from anywhere perhaps still too mainstream? What about experimental coffees? Does coffee taste better if it's cross-pollinated with tasty crops like strawberries?
- Is cross-pollination enough? Or do you get the best coffee of all if the beans are first eaten, then excreted by a particular variety of weasel?
- If weasel-excreted coffee is too disgusting, could a synthetic imitation of the weasel's digestive process (which has been created by a laboratory) be a way to enjoy the flavor while avoiding the gag reflex?

I suspect that coffee is such a constant topic of conversation because we wish to be friendly and have nothing else in common; coffee is about as deep as our shared values go.

Ecclesiastes 1:2–11 (the first reading for today) provides us with a better foundation for a relationship than coffee, and with some more usable initial premises for talking to skeptics. The book opens with despair and disillusionment, because they're what we really all have in common, regardless of our belief system. The Preacher doesn't start by trying to show that the world is an enchanted place, in which "mountains of possibilities" tower over us (the bad metaphor comes from an antisuicide poster Health Services has placed in every bathroom on our college campus). Instead, he asks us to acknowledge that everything we can ever do or try to do is incomplete and uncertain. What we really have in common is not our dreams and hopes—these differ wildly between individuals and between cultures—but that at some point we have all had our dreams and hopes destroyed. And, if we're honest with ourselves, we have to suspect that nothing we will ever attempt will make a lasting difference in this world. "All things are vanity! What profit has man from all the labor which he toils at under the sun?" (Eccl 1:2–3).

The Preacher makes assumptions that we all know to be true, even if temperamentally we would like to deny them. If we're honest, we will grant these premises, whether we are Catholic or atheist. Everything *is* tentative and uncertain, and our greatest victories are always incomplete and easily undone. We all cherish illusions and forced hopes by which we attempt to protect ourselves from the complexities of reality. Atheists are no exceptions; most commonly, their props include the inevitability of "Progress", the infallibility of science, the inherently beneficent nature of the welfare state, and the genuineness and efficacy of their own good intentions.

The first step to engaging those who live in a different metaphysical universe is for both sides to abandon these props and to face the complexity of a reality where, on the face of it, all does seem vanity. The Preacher has the courage to separate faith from forced hope, Lady Wisdom from Pollyanna. And this may be why so many people with little use for religion still ponder over Ecclesiastes.

Tuesday of the Twenty-Sixth Week in Ordinary Time
(Job 3:1–3, 11–17, 20–23)

Yesterday, in this pessimistic period of the Church year, we moved from the skepticism of Ecclesiastes to the pessimism of Job. As the book began, Job was living a life of prosperity because he had acted in accordance with God's laws. But then Job was forced to experience the contingency and uncertainty of existence in its most painful form. He lost absolutely everything: possessions, family, health, you name it. There is a reason his name is synonymous with adversity—and how to deal with it.

Yesterday's reading (Job 1:6–22) teaches that even disaster can show us the existence of God by forcibly revealing to us the contingency and impermanence of all things. All things are perpetually in the process of dissolution. But how can even dissolution or contingency be grasped and known unless we have a mental concept of something integral, unified, and essential? Our ideas are drawn from our experience—even futuristic science fiction is typically just a distorted rendering of the author's present time—and nothing in the material universe is completely integral, whole, and essential. Our very ability to mourn or lament implies the soul's elemental knowledge of God, and the image of God in man. A dog whimpers but does not properly mourn, for mourning is an act of abstraction that acknowledges both the reality of loss and the possibility that things could have been otherwise. The destruction of anything only proves its finitude, its inability to exist of itself. The finite world implies the existence of the infinite. "The Lord gave and the Lord has taken away; blessed be the name of the Lord" (Job 1:21).

The skeptical wisdom of Job and Ecclesiastes is good for October, is good for fall. It is good wisdom for Ordinary Time. These books show us how to maintain faith in the face of adversity and how to communicate faith to those who lack it. Whether we're trying to talk to others or just talk sense into ourselves in a bad situation, we shouldn't move too quickly to the optimistic side of religion: hope, comfort, and consolation. We need to be willing to linger awhile with loss and confusion, no matter how uncomfortable that might be. Job actually challenges the would-be nihilist, showing that we can't even assert that the universe lacks meaning without paying an accidental tribute to God.

But today's reading (Job 3:1–3, 11–17, 20–23) reminds me that while this argument works rationally, it doesn't necessarily make anyone feel any better. Job proceeds fairly quickly from praising God, the only self-subsistent being, and acknowledging him as the source of all subsistent being, to cursing the day he was born and wishing he didn't exist and never had existed (3, 11, 16). The proof from contingency convincingly establishes God's existence, but it doesn't establish anything about his character or about the world he created. It doesn't make you feel better, as it makes Job feel no better—except that it gives him Someone to yell at and complain to (which, I suppose, is some small consolation).

This morning, my two-year-old daughter was sitting in her high chair at breakfast when she suddenly picked a raisin out of her cereal and, exclaiming, "Look what I can do, Mama!" shoved it up her nose. It lodged there before we could extract it, and she screamed out in pain. I popped her out of her high chair and we dragged her to the bathroom, where she twisted and writhed as I held her down and Emily tried to dislodge the raisin with tweezers. But it was actually too far up to pull out. We couldn't reach it. I had to leave for work in half an hour, and we seemed to be suddenly looking at a morning in the emergency room. And Beatrice couldn't quit howling. In my panic, I irrationally summoned up the specter of death, imagining that the raisin could move from nose to throat and lodge, choking her. But after a horrible death-rattle cough and a dramatic, terrain-covering sneeze, the raisin shook loose and fell out on the bathroom floor mat.

This is a tragicomic scene of the contingency and absurdity of existence. Something as stupid as a raisin can upend our lives and make us suddenly aware of how fragile our grip on life and health are. It doesn't take an invading army to lose children. The argument from contingency for God could be established here, as in Job. But I literally shook all the way to work at an event much smaller than anything Job endured. Contingency is proof of a Creator, but it's traumatic for a creature to process fully and realize. This is the logic of Job's praise of the dead and stillborn: they are freed from contingency; they simply are or are not and do not change.

Perhaps the point here is that we need to allow people their traumas without rushing to pious consolations ("Everything happens for a reason") and we must not hide our own contingency from ourselves. Contingency is one thing we all have in common; the fragile and uncertain nature of the world is a collective experience. Contingency can be a place where dialogue can begin, between skeptics and us, and between ourselves and God.

Thursday of the Twenty-Sixth Week in Ordinary Time (Job 19:21–27)

We are nearing fall break and are in the middle of midterm exams and major paper due dates. The professorial workload spikes, and tempers worsen. Everyone loiters near the coffee maker in the photocopy room, seeking an audience for his complaint.

"Is this our promised end?" moans one colleague.

"Onward!" intones another, but with a faltering voice that turns the exclamation into a question and suggests that he would rather sink into the earth.

For the sake of conversation, I try to join in on the general whining about our work conditions, though I have no real problem with them. "As Moses might have said, it's tough making bricks without straw," I flippantly and insincerely complain.

"Do you have to bring religion into everything?" a professor colleague leaning up against the mailboxes snaps in her nasal Midwestern accent. I sigh to myself. I should have seen it coming. She and I get along nicely so long as conversation stays on our Midwestern home states and keeps away from religion. I can't be personally offended, since there is nothing personal going on here. My colleague also yells at cashiers who wish her a "blessed day"—and narrates the story later to all comers.

"Pretty much, yes," I reply. "Ban biblical allusion and you won't have much literature left to teach." But I get out of the photocopy room as soon as I can, and I'm not feeling any less alienated.

Of course, the problem is not this particular colleague; she genuinely cares about helping students (the tougher the case, the better), and we have collaborated on many projects to improve the education our department offers. The problem is that her beliefs are the norm for an American public university—she is just unusually vocal about them. Students know that in many classes in the humanities and social sciences, the easiest route to an A is to assault organized religion; they've internalized this strategy. I just had a good student turn in a paper in which he argued that Dante wrote the *Inferno* to ensure a mindless conformity to ecclesiastical power; as proof, he cited Dante's decision to put all scientists in hell. The argument is literally nonsensical. Yes, Dante put alchemists and astrologers in hell. But alchemists and astrologers aren't exactly scientists. And if Dante loved authority so much, why are there popes in his hell? The student is smarter than this, and I suspect his personal beliefs aren't involved here either. He is no militant atheist or progressive idealist; he is a jovially cynical frat boy with a fake tan. He is doubtless responding to training from previous professors, seeking, as always, the quickest path to the high grade he usually earns.

So how can I talk about ultimate things with people to whom the very mention of God is offensive?

Today, the Church recommends epistemological humility.

The Bible's skeptical wisdom, emphasized in Ordinary Time, reaches people by stripping away preconception and cliché. We face a universe that we can't fully comprehend, whose existence and nature are troublingly contingent and uncertain, whose Maker (if any) cannot be known by us in any empirical sense because by the nature of the case he couldn't be defined or conceived.

The sin of Job's friends, as Job puts it many times, is their effort to stand in for God: "Why do you hound me as though you were divine, and insatiably prey upon me?" (Job 19:22, from today's first reading, Job 19:21–27). It's difficult to think meaningfully about our own finitude, to have the chastened wisdom, the wistful sympathy, of a Job or an Ecclesiastes. This is the beginning of wisdom, but we recoil, wishing for a simpler account of the universe, even if it is less true. With Job's friends, this takes the form of religious cliché. Their efforts to defend God ultimately discredit God by making God seem both finite and unjust.

The impulse to simplify the universe can take other, less theistic forms. A materialistic consumer lives in a very simple universe with an obvious order (capitalism) and rewards (getting money) and punishments (losing money).

An atheistic believer in popular science thinks he lives in a defined and knowable universe of simple laws (though actual science concludes otherwise). These are all attempts to take shelter from our human condition. If we honor God, we must admit the complexity of the universe and stand with Job against his friends. God speaks, in the end, only to those who refuse to render him finite, to Job, not his comforters.

One of my favorite colleagues is a soft-spoken, extremely affable agnostic. "Agnostic" may even be too definite a term. He is either a theistic agnostic or an agnostic the-ist, too sympathetic toward theism to be a good agnostic, and too agnostic to be a good theist. He delights in how his approach to religion confuses students, who are used to spending English classes either agreeing or disagreeing with the professor's beliefs. "Since they can't figure out what I think, they're placed in the awkward position of thinking for themselves," he observes. He is a proud fam-ily man, and he has a child with developmental disabili-ties. Since I'm now a parent myself, and the mention of children can sometimes shut down faculty conversation, he discusses his life with me over (of course) coffee in a campus-area bakery.

My colleague is a good friend, and he may even be my doppelganger. I can't see it myself, but eighteen-year-old students find us identical and accidentally call us by each other's names (short hair, glasses, average height, thin, professional dress—this is all the resemblance it takes, I guess). But his life is filled with questions that I have never faced, such as whether a home and nearby institutions are sufficiently accessible, or whether the care is adequate and affordable in a particular area. He resides sixty miles from our college, in part because his child needs facilities found only in a major metro area. I can't begin to fathom or to claim to understand the joys and sorrows of his life. I don't know what to say.

So I just listen to his story and lend him a book by the Methodist theologian Stanley Hauerwas and recommend another by the Jesuit thinker Father Henri Nouwen. These authors have worked with and written about the developmentally disabled. They depict how all of us precisely because of our brokenness and our limitations can be channels of grace. And they don't attempt to explain away or legitimate our brokenness, pain, and confusion. They are no Job's comforters. They simply show us the divine life and invite us to enter in.

Twenty-Seventh Sunday in Ordinary Time
(Mk 10:2–16)

I am the father of a two-year-old daughter. The meditation the father of a young child should make on today's Gospel—the story of Jesus asking, over the protests of his disciples, that the children come unto him (Mk 10:2–16)—is fairly obvious. I should write about the wonders of children and how much we can learn from them. It's one of the most commonly rendered—and one of the most sentimentalized—scenes in Scripture.

But I'm in a contrarian mood this morning. So can't a word be said for the disciples? Jesus is in the middle of a debate with his enemies, the Pharisees. Exactly how often and under what circumstances a person could ethically divorce was a contentious issue, then as now. The Pharisees are trying to discredit Jesus by putting him in a position where whatever he says will anger a large sector of the population. American Catholics should understand this, if anyone can. Whenever the Church tries to speak up in favor of stable homes and permanent marriages, she is decried as unpastoral, insensitive to the divorced. Whenever the Church tries to show pastoral sensitivity to the divorced by applying her own norms as generously as she can, then she is decried as hypocritical for running "annulment mills". There is still nothing to be said about the subject of divorce that won't cause an outcry. The Pharisees provoke one of the most profound divine statements about the nature of marriage (it is utterly permanent, a bond that can't be broken, a bond that echoes the nature of the unfallen world), but they didn't do this really intending to learn anything about marriage; it was a simple trap.

So, as Jesus is in the middle of this complicated debate-ambush with some of the most astute debaters and reasoners of his time, up comes a mob of children. If there is one thing we can grant about children, it's that they don't help to clarify debate or to keep a conversation on topic. Children are the natural enemies of orderly forward progress. Our local mall is so small that it's always on the verge of going out of business. But if I don't know what to do and I need to kill an hour, I can always just get my daughter to try to walk from one end of it to the other. She'll zigzag sideways more often than straight; she'll climb into and out of every empty chair in the food court and each rental shopping cart with a cartoon character on it; she will grab and maul all mannequins, peer into each window, and ascend and descend the mall's two escalators (which she calls "alligators") many times. Children stand entirely in the way of an orderly progression from point A to point B. They're the last people you want rushing the stage when you're in the middle of a complicated debate with a hostile audience. The nation is now in the middle of a presidential election; the first debate was last week. Both candidates have spent a lot of time on the trail kissing babies. But I note they did not allow a bunch of little kids to rush the stage during the debate.

Perhaps this is in part Jesus' point. The Kingdom of God is not governed by Occam's razor and is not to be sought as the most efficient means of moving from point A to point B. Its progression is not linear, and while its truths are logically defensible, they are not to be discovered by debate. Jesus' answer to the Pharisees transcends anything in Mosaic law; technically speaking, the Pharisees are on better exegetical ground. The Kingdom of God is the experience of glory and the ineffable; viewed in temporal terms, its path is always zigzagging.

Today I was able to take Beatrice to a Mass with a children's Liturgy of the Word. The children colored pictures of themselves, then taped their pictures up by a picture of Jesus, to fit the Gospel. The pictures ended up in all angles askew, and Beatrice's picture was literally a series of purple zigzags. For such is the Kingdom of heaven.

Twenty-Eighth Sunday in Ordinary Time
(Ps 90:12–13, 14–15, 16–17)

Today's Responsorial Psalm (Ps 90:12–13, 14–15, 16–17) requests that God would "teach us to number our days aright, that we may gain wisdom of heart" (12). Dorothy Sayers, the great Anglican novelist and theologian, realized that this Psalm possessed a vision of wisdom that flies in the face of twentieth- (and twenty-first)-century common sense. Her most famous literary creation, the charmingly agnostic fictional detective Lord Peter Wimsey, found it particularly chilling and appalling. Upon encountering Psalm 90—and the very similar Psalm 39—in the Anglican funeral service, he shuddered and remarked that he certainly hoped he wouldn't know the number of his days; it would make it too hard to live in the meantime.[1]

Modern Western culture is marked especially by a penchant perpetually to remake and reshape the world we live in, to treat ourselves as protean, entirely permeable beings in no real way subject to death. If we accept that we are mortal and that we are finite, what would be more reasonable than to pray that we would know our number of days? We would wish to have a sense of the time allotted to us, so that we might use this time wisely and redemptively and be ready to lay our lives down when the time comes. But the first step here is one that culturally we cannot take: acknowledging our own mortality, granting that we have a finite number of days, that there are limits.

Friends and coworkers have yelled at me recently for calling my now forty-year-old self "middle-aged". How can this be offensive, I wonder, when it is precisely statistically accurate (according to the World Health Organization, the overall life expectancy for the United States is 79.8 years)? I suppose my self-designation as middle-aged must be offensive only because it suggests that life has a middle, and if there is a middle, then there must be an end ...

In 2006, I got a paper about the September 11, 2001, terrorist attacks from a college freshman. The paper explicitly advocated genocide for Muslims, going on at gruesome length and in excruciating detail about how we should bomb and kill all inhabitants of devoutly Islamic countries. The author was a pretty blond girl fond of wearing sweatshirts with Disney characters on them. She dressed like an unusually sheltered ten-year-old and wrote like an exceptionally violent mercenary. I could make no sense of it.

---

[1] See *The Nine Tailors* (San Diego: Harvest/Harcourt, 1934), section 2, part 3.

As she revised her paper and discussed it with me in conferences, she gradually revealed that until September 11, her parents had refused to let her view any movie that involved death, failed to tell her about any family funerals, and even lied to her about the death of family pets. And when the 9/11 attacks occurred, she was thirteen! She turned thirteen in a world where death did not exist. Her desire to kill Muslims was a traumatized reaction to the shattering of the deathless Disneyland in which she lived, where she was an immortal fairy princess and Walt Disney would one day awake from his cryogenic slumber. And she had learned no wisdom from the experience. She seemed to think that if every Islamic person could be killed, then her fairy world would be restored. She is one example among thousands of the destructive character of the contemporary rejection of human finitude. Children are not to be told of it, adults are to be distracted from it, even the elderly are not to speak of it. And this is vicious, violent, and deadly. If we do not number our days, we remain in ignorance and malform our nature.

Here's to middle age and to counting the days!

Monday of the Twenty-Eighth Week in Ordinary Time
(Lk 11:29–32)

Luke 11:29 is haunting: "This generation ... seeks a sign, but no sign will be given it, except the sign of Jonah." In other words, no sign will be given but the ultimate sign, the impossible sign, the sign that contains all other signs. The great sea creature—such as the whale that swallowed Jonah—is associated with the sea monster Leviathan and is, like the ocean, a symbol in the Hebrew Scriptures for primordial chaos. Going under the water is associated with death. The third day is the day of God's action. No sign will be given, then, except the return of life from the dead, of order from chaos. No sign will be given except the ultimate sign that permits all other signs to have meaning. No significance will be given except ultimate significance. Nothing will have meaning except everything.

And Jesus utters these amazing words not in an inspiring speech but in a frustrated and angry lecture. The point of the passage as a whole (Lk 11:29–32, today's Gospel reading) is that what he is saying doesn't matter because no one is going to get it. Something greater than Solomon and Jonah is there—but no one will see or notice. The ultimate sign will be written—but most people will find it illegible. Perhaps it is illegible because it's written in letters too large. The people of this evil generation are essentially standing right under the Hollywood sign in California, or six inches away from a pointillist painting. What we can see and read depends on perspective and on cultural convention.

If we've decided that nothing transcendent exists, that only what is material is real, and that there are no universal truths, then signs can be read only within these bounds. The lesser miracles or smaller divine signs can be made to fit these limits. If Jesus multiplies the loaves and fishes, we can enjoy the food while denying its meaning (Jesus probably had a cart full of the stuff hidden out back, but it's still nice of him to share). If Jesus heals the sick, we can appreciate the result, even if we question the cause (most illnesses are just in people's minds anyway, so it's great that he made people feel better). The Church's unbounded work for the poor is a present-day miraculous sign. People aren't naturally generous or self-sacrificial; generally, they help others only because the government coerces them to do so through taxes. The Church's worldwide social-welfare network is a visible sign of God's presence in the world. But again, the sign can be made to fit our narrow and cynical view of the world (the Church helps the poor only to perpetuate her own power and influence, but it's still nice that the poor are being fed). In short, the miraculous sign can be accepted so long as it can be made to conform to and support the world as we already conceive it: a closed system, a purely material entity, manageable by politics, ruled by power, predictable in its events and outcomes.

What is precisely unacceptable is the restoration of life, for this would shatter every last one of our assumptions and cause us to rethink everything. The Resurrection cannot be made to conform to the world as we conceive it; the event itself is objectionable, not merely the interpretation. The only sign that will be given is precisely the sign that cannot—that must not—ever be read and accepted. There is no sign, because we have been given the ultimate sign.

Saturday of the Twenty-Ninth Week in Ordinary Time
(Eph 4:7–16)

On Wednesday, we spent five hours interviewing candidates for Catholic campus minister for my university. The diocesan head of Campus and Young Adult Ministry chaired the group, assisted by the Protestant chaplain, the deacon from the local parish, two student leaders from the campus ministry, and one faculty representative (me). One interview was conducted (awkwardly) by cell phone; each of us slid the cell phone down the plastic cafeteria table in the parish hall to who was to ask the next question. Most of the other interviews were conducted (only slightly less awkwardly) from the same location via Skype. Thanks to Skype, one interviewee spent the whole interview speaking not to the hiring committee but to a giant bottle of Pepsi we had accidentally placed in front of the camera. I hate Skype.

In today's epistle (Eph 4:7–16), Paul expounds the spiritual gifts involved in leadership. God has given the Church a variety of ministerial gifts in a descending hierarchy (first apostles, then prophets, etc.), none of which is to be treated as an end in itself or a source of personal power. All gifts exist "for building up the Body of Christ"; they bring us individually to psychological and spiritual stability and maturity and collectively to "unity of the faith" (12, 13). And, all in all, the interview experience gave me hope for the direction of the Church; our job candidates illustrate this passage without irony. We interviewed a soft-spoken Notre Dame graduate who identifies "hospitality" as his spiritual gift and imagines campus ministry as a house ever open. We interviewed a self-described charismatic Catholic with a beard and an earring who works at a Catholic camp and retreat center, where he plays the guitar in a praise band. We interviewed a married couple in which the brunette wife combined a deep devotion to the Little Flower with the perky personality of a sorority girl, and the crew-cut husband possessed the soft-spoken gravity of an undertaker. And the list goes on. Although each of these people was entirely different in approach, and we can ultimately hire only one, I am certain that each has a life ahead of him building up the body of Christ.

I have been thinking lately about the importance of accepting our limits—our mortality, our insufficiency—if we are to quit fantasizing and be of real service to Christ and the Church. You can exercise any gift effectively only after you've quit pretending that you have them all. Before that point, you may mean well, but you're just a dreamer, and your dreams are not untainted by hubris; you haven't yet realized that other people are used by God in ways that you yourself simply are not, that you need other people. Wednesday's interviews unexpectedly confronted me with my own limitations yet again.

Most serious Catholics have considered at one point or another whether they might possess a religious vocation. In my early twenties, I spent two years discerning a possible vocation, though I never entered formation. Shortly after completing my bachelor of arts, I was accepted as a postulant by a religious order but declined the invitation at the last second. I then spent a very depressed year working midnights at a fast-food restaurant, after which I went to graduate school for English, earned a Ph.D., became a professor, and now assist the campus ministry. Like probably anyone who has considered the priesthood and didn't ultimately seek ordination, I sometimes am haunted by fantasies that, with a little more holiness and self-control, I could have served God in the highest of all possible ways. Saint Chene the Evangelist is a favorite fantasy self of mine.

For the first half of one of our Skype interviews today, I kept wondering, "What's that behind that guy's head? Where is he?" His profile was framed on the right by a strange tan rectangle and on the left by a fuzzy gray protrusion that looked like a disheveled Muppet. Midway through the interview, I realized that I was looking at a corkboard and an industrial mop. At my fast-food restaurant we had an identical corkboard (for posting notifications and reminders) and an identical mop. I looked down at the candidate's résumé and saw that our interviewee now works at a fast-food restaurant.

I suddenly put it together: this guy—with his flat brown hair, glasses, and stodgy gray suit—was Skyping on his break at the restaurant. We were interviewing my shadow self, a fast-food employee with clerical aspirations. His résumé told the story. He had looked into being a priest and studied at seminary, failed to complete seminary, then was unemployed for a year; joined a full-time volunteer campus missions program, then quit; then was unemployed for another year. Now he works at a fast-food restaurant. And in his awkwardness, palpable depression, and self-hate, it was clear quickly that he couldn't get our job either. His love for God was plain, and emotionally I wanted to give him a job, but students would have run away from him screaming.

I was actually deeply shaken by interviewing him. I prayed earnestly that night that he would discover his gifts and know how he should serve God and the world. I prayed also for myself, thanking God that I had been given another important lesson in accepting my finitude. Here was a much more likely outcome for me than Saint Chene the Evangelist if I hadn't gotten my doctorate and gotten married: to be a spiritual will-o'-the-wisp, forever vacillating between religious and secular life, hovering on the fringes of both, of use to neither, devoid of peace. Part of accepting one's place in the body of Christ is accepting one's gifts and doing what one can to build up the body, whatever it is. Out of fantasy, into actuality.

8

LESSONS IN APOCALYPTIC LIVING
(Ordinary Time, Round 2, Part 4)

Thirtieth Sunday in Ordinary Time
(Ps 126:1–2, 2–3, 4–5, 6)

Today's Responsorial Psalm (Ps 126:1–2, 2–3, 4–5, 6) opens with an evocative image: the captives of Zion, now restored to their land, are "like men dreaming" (1). Dreams are distinguished from waking life mostly in that their events or logic violate our sense of reality in some subtle way. Dreams possess something of the flavor of reality—people and incidents from our daily life factor in, and there is some sort of sequence and causal logic—but something is slightly off. People are present in places where they would never actually be; causes are not correspondent with their effects. I awoke from a nightmare yesterday morning and had to lie in bed for thirty minutes before I figured out that the events in it had not happened, before I was able to trace the thread that revealed its unreality.

My dream was likely triggered by the kitchen renovation that will start tomorrow. The remodel is the result of our decision to stay and make this house work rather than buy some giant fantasy house (for the first time, we will have a dishwasher, adequate cabinet space, and, since an island wouldn't fit, a peninsula). In my dream, a short guy with sandy hair in a muscle T-shirt pulled up in front of our house in a pickup truck. I initially ignored him, since pickup trucks are not uncommon on our street (we live in the Appalachian South, after all). Then he knocked on the door and offered to fix our screen porch. I told him there was nothing wrong with it, and he asked me to look at it. As I looked at it, I saw that the screens had been ripped and the wood had been gouged, rather obviously in the last few minutes by the man who stood in front of me. I made my accusations, and he calmly replied, "Sure looks like it needs fixed, however it happened." And then he waited for me to pay him.

It took my sleepy mind time to sort this through, since I do distrust contractors, having been overcharged by them before (in fact, by a fellow not unlike the figure in my dream). The dream is an exaggerated version of my picture of reality, and so it took time to uncover the distortion.

If the restored captives—and, by extension, all of us whom Christ has restored—are like "men dreaming", this says something of their (and our) overall picture of reality. We don't really envision reality in terms of our faith. Our (or at least my) gut-level definition of reality is a Darwinian, empty, mechanistic universe. When God acts as faith asserts he will act—the restoration of the captives to Israel had been long prophesied, like our redemption by Christ—we merely respond "like men dreaming". For God's redemptive action just doesn't line up with our skewed sense of reality. It takes awhile for us really to begin to reorient our thinking, to wake up and realize that *previously* we were dreaming, and *now* we are seeing the world as it really is. I pray that one day this truth fully dawns on me, and I can wake up once and for all.

Commemoration of All the Faithful Departed
(All Souls' Day, November 2) (Wis 3:1–9)

Each All Souls' Day, Saint Hedwig's Cemetery in Dearborn, Michigan—less than a mile from my mother's house—lights candles on top of each grave. Since the cemetery occupies about a square mile in an otherwise highly developed area, the sight seems surreal. The nondescript state highway (Ford Road, Michigan 153) strewn with gas stations and strip malls suddenly becomes the Dead Marshes of J. R. R. Tolkien's Middle Earth, as your path is literally lit by the dead. And, as in Tolkien, the lights could prove a snare: it is very hard to keep your eyes on the road and focus on traffic when your peripheral vision is weirdly aglow.

My Irish Catholic grandmother, Gertrude Fox, is buried in St. Hedwig's Cemetery and is one of these shining souls. She was also the first dead person for whom I ever prayed. She died just before Christmas while I was taking RCIA (Rite of Christian Initiation of Adults) classes, intending to convert to Catholicism the following Easter. Shortly after her funeral, I bundled myself in a heavy trench coat and fought the snow to make it to Mass at the west side Detroit parish she had attended. After Mass, I lit a candle in the rack in front of the statues of the saints. I prayed for her as Pentecostals are taught to pray: head bowed, eyes closed, arms outstretched. When I opened my eyes, I saw that the flame of my candle had impossibly grown to four times the size of that of the other candles. I was astounded: I was witnessing a miracle, a divine sign that my prayers had been answered and my grandmother had passed directly into heaven. Then I moved my arm and found a much more material explanation: my trench coat was on fire. My grandmother would have enjoyed the scene.

Gertrude Fox was a woman for whom faith was a waking reality. She possessed no pious sentiment—or sentimentality of any kind. Those who did possess it she mocked as "holier than God". As far as she was concerned, faith was simply a proposition about reality that was true. Sentiment was beside the point. She thought of herself as liberal and liked to mock traditionalists, but her terms were set in the 1950s, and while her manner was iconoclastic, her operating assumptions were orthodox. She had a biting wit, and would give you the shirt off her back and then make fun of how it looked on you. She worked a full-time job until she was seventy-eight, and lived in the city of Detroit long after our family had fled to the suburbs. When in a single night neighbors on each side of her were robbed, everyone expected her to be traumatized. She just shrugged. "Every night I pray for God to protect me, and I expect him to do it," she muttered. She dealt with widowhood and a changing world rationally, practically, and without the slightest bit of escapism. She gave me the sense that faith was a bedrock assumption that squared with reality, and she may have had a larger role in my becoming Catholic than Augustine of Hippo or Blaise Pascal did, though pompous bookish sort that I am, I would not have acknowledged it at the time (and may not acknowledge it often enough even now).

As a lector at her funeral, I read today's Old Testament reading about the faithful departed (Wis 3:1–9). Since hers was my first Catholic funeral, these words will be forever associated for me with my grandmother. Like the scriptural author, Gertrude Fox mocks as superficial and foolish those who think she has perished (2)—and heaven help the mortal skeptic willing to provoke her wit.

Saturday of the Thirtieth Week in Ordinary Time
(Phil 1:18b–26)

No one likes "indifference" anymore. The term is now invariably pejorative, just as the term "passionate" is always positive. The object of this passion (or this indifference) doesn't matter at all. My students have sympathy with the person who is passionate about politics and with the person who is passionate about religion and with the person who is passionate about partying. A heightened emotional intensity is all that matters. When a former student conducted a survey of faculty in my department, she excitedly asked each of us, "What are you passionate about?" I shocked her by replying, "I am not a passionate person."

Paul in today's first reading (Phil 1:18b–26) is the opposite of my students. He is the master of indifference. He is indifferent to what seems to most of us the ultimate question: literally, life or death. But he is quite certain about his object: Christ. "For me life is Christ and death is gain.... And I do not know which I shall choose" (21, 22).

Faith is subject to two common attacks. Sigmund Freud makes both of them, though they are contradictory. The first is that faith is life-denying; the putative desire for eternal life in heaven is actually a desire for death. Only a corpse escapes the uncertainty, change, and vagaries of material existence; all desire for stasis is a death drive. The second is that faith is a form of wish fulfillment. The faithful love life so much that they cannot accept the reality of death and instead delude themselves that they are eternal. The difficult trick in trying to argue with these objections is that they are mutually exclusive. If you argue that as a Christian you really love life, then you must be guilty of wish fulfillment; if you argue that you are not so delusional as to deny the definitive nature of death, then you must have a death drive.

Of course, we all know (and perhaps ourselves have been) Christians who justify these ideas. The 1980s Christian punk rock T-shirt with a smiley face surrounded by crossbones read, "Die Happy". My sister owned one. There are also sentimental Christians who can't stand the mention of difficulty, death, darkness, or suffering, anything that could get in the way of wish fulfillment and fantasy; someone bought all those Thomas Kincaid reproductions and Precious Moments figurines.

But Paul has refuted Freud's ideas without ever hearing them. Freud cannot imagine genuine indifference; the person who seeks life and the person who seeks death are equally passionate. Paul, however, is so certain of Christ that he doesn't care whether he lives or dies. Christ has broken down the life-death binary; they are no longer set categories. Christ has conquered death through death, and redefined life. In Christ, life and death are no longer divided, and can both be taken lightly.

Wednesday of the Thirty-First Week in Ordinary Time (Phil 2:12–18; Lk 14:25–33)

Paul writes in today's epistle (Phil 2:12–18) about the only matter we should never treat with indifference: we must "work out [our] salvation in fear and trembling" (12). This passage isn't discussed much anymore, probably because it mentions fear. The fear of God is now rarely considered a virtue, associated as it is with the image of a manipulative God of wrath.

But, of course, we do worry about things we care about. People sit up nights wondering, "Does she love me or love me not?" They lose their appetites as they await the results of a job interview. They run their health into the ground for advancement at work. Novelists ruin relationships and harm their families in their obsession with getting the story right. I spent nine years in graduate school, living below the federal poverty line while working more than sixty hours a week, since I cared about the subject matter and wanted to be a professor. Whatever we care about, we work out in fear and trembling. It's no surprise that Søren Kierkegaard chose this phrase as a book title. To work out something in fear and trembling is to live existentially in faith, to live in a state of ultimate concern.

Today's Gospel (Lk 14:25–33) makes a similar point: "If any one comes to me without hating his father and mother, wife and children, brothers and sisters, and even his own life, he cannot be my disciple" (27). It sounds harsh to say that we don't care about Christ if we don't give things and people up for him. But if we do care about him at all, then this will happen; we will lose friends and possessions over anything we care about. Friends drifted away because I had to leave the state of Michigan for graduate school and, later, work. A misguided acquaintance who believes in marijuana rights lost a job because he refused to submit to a drug test. Another has spent a life working as a dishwasher because he won't cut his hair ("It's who I am. People just can't handle who I am," he explained as we both worked back in a restaurant kitchen). People make sacrifices for things they care about—whatever those things happen to be. This is not God being harsh; this is the nature of a finite universe, where we cannot choose all goods simultaneously. As Søren Kierkegaard and Blaise Pascal both emphasize, faith is ultimately a question of choice, and the nature of reality won't permit us not to choose. We will inevitably live our lives in fear and trembling and self-sacrifice—the only question, really, is whether we will find salvation.

What we don't approach with fear and trembling are things we don't care about. I am willing to grant in the abstract that I should probably exercise. In 2005, for about two weeks, I occasionally did sit-ups. Prior to that, I last exercised for about a week in 1987. My interest in my health and physique does not reach a level of ultimate concern. I hope that I don't become ill as I get older, but the question frankly isn't sufficiently interesting to me to generate any action. I don't worry about it, when it comes down to it. I tell my students that I get sufficient exercise from pacing while I lecture and from participating in the rotation of the earth upon its axis. I feel no fear or trembling and possess no ultimate concern. So there is no action.

Ordinary Time is chock-full of Pauline readings, and Paul is a perfect companion for this season of the liturgical year. He is a shrewd observer of human psychology, calling us out of the places where we would endeavor to hide and very practically pointing out to us the next destination we need spiritually to reach and how to get there. The time between Ascension and Advent can seem vacant; it's easy to substitute "Empty Time" for Ordinary Time. Paul famously compares the spiritual life to a marathon, and he is a sage coach on the long race of Ordinary Time.

Saturday of the Thirty-First Week in Ordinary Time (Lk 16:9–15)

In today's Gospel (Lk 16:9–15), Jesus tells us scandalously to "make friends with dishonest wealth", to gain eternity through money (9). His irony is exquisite. Typically, people use others, manipulating and taking advantage of their tastes and weaknesses, in order to make money. People are the means, and money is the end. Followers of Christ, however, are to reverse this dynamic. We are to take advantage of and manipulate money to benefit others and our own soul. Money is the means, and people (and their eternal good) are the end. This takes some training and some reorientation of our thinking.

You don't become a master manipulator overnight. Even a skilled con man must use and manipulate a person gradually and by degrees. He must first really seem like a friend, win the mark's trust, and then slowly and imperceptibly begin turning his aims in other directions, leaving the now-established relationship seemingly intact, a hollow shell that can be exploited. This is often what passes for "professional networking". And the process applies even to manipulating money.

Over the course of this year, my wife and I have been trying to learn to get the better of money. In addition to our tithe to the Church, we have bought meals for college students and have paid their bills, rent, and graduate school application fees, as well as for their car repairs (rent typically is the largest expense). We have always said, "This is what money is for," but each time, some part of me resents the expenditure. We could have gone out for dinner with that money, or gone on vacation, or even just sped up the timetable for paying off the house. But as the liturgical year hits me time and time again with the teachings of Jesus, I do really begin to believe that helping others is what money is for, and to feel some repulsion at thoughts of excess. Gradually, one does come to mean what one says, and gradually one's thoughts begin to accord with one's own actions.

Friday of the Thirty-Second Week in Ordinary Time
(Lk 17:26–37)

As the Church year comes to an end, the liturgical readings emphasize the apocalypse, the end times, the Last
Things. In today's Gospel reading from Luke (17:26–37),
Jesus explains how surprisingly easy it is for us to miss the
apocalypse—the ultimate meaning of everything, the end
of the world. He gives a series of cautionary examples
(26–29) that illustrate the triumph of the mundane over
apocalyptic vision. In the days of Noah, people marry and
are given in marriage while missing the event that actually
defines the nature of their times—the Flood. They are psychologically antediluvian, even as they drown. In Sodom,
more damningly, they eat, drink, buy, and sell; their time
is structured according to the rhythms of pleasure and
commerce. And as a result, they miss the fire that burns
them all. The same message is applied to us, as we are
told that, when the end comes, we should not to go back
into the house for our goods (31); we should hold all things
lightly in view of the end.

In texts like this, the Church is reminding us what the
liturgical year is about. If the Anglican poet and theologian
Christina Rossetti is right, then liturgical time is apocalyptic time, a training in how to discern ultimate meaning
and final meaning.[1] Our experience of liturgical time
should be altering and shaping our means of perception,
the very way we see the world. Jesus said, "The light
of the body is the eye: if therefore thy eye be single, thy
whole body shall be full of light" (Mt 6:22, KJV). If this is
so, in reshaping our perceptions, we will be altering and

---

[1] See her book *Called to Be Saints: The Minor Festivals Devotionally Studied*
(London: SPCK, 1893).

reshaping our very selves as well. I pray that as this year ends, I might be learning how to live apocalyptically, how to exist in Christ's Kingdom.

Saturday of the Thirty-Second Week in Ordinary Time
(3 Jn 5–8)

Today was our parish's designated "Helping Hands Day". First, I and many others spent three hours working at our church. We bagged hundreds of meals for the hungry on an assembly line of folding tables. A middle-aged mother barked orders with a smile as helpers ranging from her own elementary-school-aged children to parishioners too old to lift the food they had bagged assisted in their own ways. Then we took it all down to the local soup kitchen. This task finished early, so then I found myself precariously sweeping leaves off of the roof of Tabor Retreat Center, quite uncertain how I would get down again after jumping onto the roof from a stepladder. Others made cards or did yard work for the shut-ins, took food to the Salvation Army, and so on.

I rode to the soup kitchen with a man nearing eighty, a former Navy pilot, a former electrical technician, who is bored and depressed now that his wife has died and compensates by filling his days with acts of charity. He drove an enormous old van, which he steered with the precision of a pilot. He insisted on having his Garmin GPS navigator direct us, even though we knew where we were going. Between the machine's ignorance of road construction and the man's difficulty hearing the machine, it took us at least twice as long to get back to the church as it ought to have. Every time the Garmin gave directions in its high-pitched electronic voice, he replied, "Whatever you say, lady," and took the turn whether it made sense or not; he was equally amused with the joke each time. In the passenger seat, I thought back to the isolation and disconnection from my parish that I felt at the beginning of this year, and wondered how I came to find myself now being piloted by a man I had never met to who knows where. Back at the church, the old man made a visit to the Blessed Sacrament, then went on his way.

In today's epistle reading (3 Jn 5–8), Saint John the Evangelist describes the early Church: "Beloved, you are faithful in all you do for the brothers and sisters, especially for strangers; they have testified to your love before the Church" (5–6). Today, our parish lived out this verse— caring for brothers and sisters, especially strangers—and I encountered a wonderful example of what it means to live in Christ's love before the Church. If I can be half the Catholic at eighty that this former Navy pilot is—giving of himself out of his emptiness, joking even in depression, ever present before Christ in the sacrament—I will have achieved something remarkable. I will have lived a life charged with meaning and full of grace.

Thirty-Third Sunday in Ordinary Time
(Dan 12:1–3; Mk 13:24–32)

I began this narrative feeling like my life was trivial and meaningless. I have made progress, I think, over the course of the year at noticing what is in front of me and seeing significance in the patterns in my life. I've gotten there, insofar as I *have* gotten there, by reading each day in light of the Scripture assigned to that day in the Church calendar.

But some weeks it still doesn't work. Some weeks I am still overwhelmed with the sense that my life is meaningless and everything I do is rote, trivial, and mundane. Take, for example, the two aspects of my life most likely to possess inherent meaning: teaching and parenting. Teaching is a noble profession, and I do really care about helping students express themselves more effectively and think more clearly; sometimes I can help give a person a chance at succeeding in life that he wouldn't have had otherwise. But right now, I spend most of my time not helping students but writing voluminous accreditation reports.[2] To make matters worse, lately I've had laryngitis. I'm too stubborn to cancel class, but I literally can't speak. So I stand in front of the class and write discussion questions on the board with a marker, and I try to weave students' answers together into some kind of coherent whole by enthusiastic pointing and dramatic hand gestures. Essentially, we've spent the week playing academic charades. I haven't been lazy; I've done my job. But heaven knows what good anyone got out of it.

Likewise, parenthood. I love my daughter, and I especially love her constant, unpredictable, sometimes-inspired speech. But lately she has discovered the song "The Wheels on the Bus". And she loves it. I mean really loves it. Loves it too much for human endurance. The song is a linguistic weed, choking out all the other words she has spent the last year learning. So Beatrice's constant speech continues—and any silence in which I could collect my thoughts remains elusive—but it no longer means anything. I'm delighted when she breaks from a verse to analyze a textual variant—"Daddy, do the wipers go 'swish'

---

[2] Note for any reader who wants even minor plot threads resolved: In the end, I did more or less miraculously figure out what we needed to do to pull off the accreditation project and somehow got volunteers to help me do it. We passed with flying colors, and I gleefully tore up each of my Tom's calendars. But that's another liturgical year, and another story.

or 'click'? I've heard both"—because at least it means that the song stops for a second. Like the baby on the bus, I am ready to go, "Waa, waa, waa." Is this, I wonder, what parenthood means?

And sometimes this feeling of boredom or ennui even extends to our decision to be open to a second child. Emily became pregnant with Beatrice something like a week after we abandoned Natural Family Planning. We're used to immediate results. Now it's been months since we made our decision, and the wondering and the waiting are growing dull. Emily has purchased a giant box of pregnancy tests and, in her desire for certainty and for empirical data, uses one every time she wonders about her cycle. But so far, nothing. "I knew it, cracked cistern," she says. "No, dry reed," I reply. And the very act of looking at a pregnancy test—surely one of the more dramatic moments in life for many couples—begins to grow tedious and anticlimactic.

On weeks like this one, I feel that I have tried to restore a sense of meaning to my life by meditating daily on the liturgical readings—but I have failed. Today, however, the Church slaps me in the face with a strong rejoinder: I don't have to *try* to craft a sense of meaning for my life. For, as today's first reading from Daniel (12:1–3) states plainly, we have no option but for our lives to possess eternal significance. This is part of being a creature with a soul, who can think, who can make decisions. Our lives have eternally positive or eternally negative consequences, both for our own souls (which, being immortal, cannot die) and for the world. We don't have the option of being merely material, of being merely mundane; we can lead others to justice and "shine brightly like the splendor of the firmament", or we can "be an everlasting horror and disgrace" both to ourselves and others

(2–3). We don't have the option of not mattering. We don't have the option of being merely trivial or merely material. We exist eternally, and we become part of the road map by which others navigate their way through this world.

So why, then, do I so often feel like everything is trivial and pointless and doesn't matter? The reading from Daniel implies the answer: I'm unconsciously seeking a dodge, an evasion. If I can convince myself that my life has no significance, I am also freed from responsibility. If nothing I do matters, then I need not take anything I do seriously. There is a relief in pretending to live as a mere animal, even if that animal is a pack animal or a workhorse. I also can disdain everything that I fail to do. What is the point of filing reports, changing diapers, or raking leaves off the retreat center roof (though if I fail to rake them, the roof collapses and whatever moment of mystical insight someone might have had in the retreat house won't happen)? If nothing matters, I am free to act or not act as I please. And it gets better: by acting like this sense of meaninglessness is something that external forces have imposed on me by the tedium of their demands, I can avoid ever realizing that it is actually a defense against God that I have erected for myself.

But, as G. K. Chesterton observed in *Heretics*, the truth is really that there are no tedious objects or tasks, only tedious people. The end result of this year of meditation is to have my means of evasion stripped away and to stand before God. And every time we stand unveiled before God, we face the Day of the Lord, the apocalypse, described in the Gospel reading (Mk 13:24–32). The final Day of the Lord at the end of time is only the ultimate rendering of this event, which occurs continually, each day in every liturgical year.

Wednesday of the Thirty-Third Week in Ordinary Time
(Rev 4:1–11)

Today, the workmen finished our kitchen remodel. Since we had to avoid being home (our small house had seven people working in it, blocking both exits), we went to the mall to look at Christmas stuff (something we normally wouldn't do until after Thanksgiving). Beatrice remains obsessed with escalators, and Macy's proudly boasts one of our tiny mall's two escalators. So we spent a couple of hours stuck in Macy's: ten times up and down the escalator and ten times around the Christmas decorations. As we went up and down the escalator over and over, I felt like an extra from some bad eighties movie; Beatrice was even dressed in a period-appropriate black-and-white dress with thick horizontal stripes and a hot pink star across the chest. We bought a sum total of one Christmas ornament, a tan porcelain dog that caught Beatrice's fancy because she thinks it looks like the golden lab up the street, a female misnamed Marley (or, as she would say, "Mawley").

Beatrice spent the ride home from the store making the dog dance on her head as she delivered speeches and sang songs about it. Before we reached the house, "Mawley is so beautiful!" and "Look at Mawley jump, Mommy! Jump, Mawley, jump!" inevitably transformed into "The Mawley on the bus goes jump, jump, jump." She was in one of toddlerhood's many small elations. But then, as she struggled to step over the threshold, Bea tripped and dropped the dog on the ground; its legs broke off. Somehow, she didn't notice that the dog's legs were gone before we rushed her off to dinner and then to bed.

After she fell asleep, I drove back to Macy's to try to buy an identical ornament so she wouldn't realize what happened and begin living in a world of loss and pain. I ran through the store in what felt like slow motion—another bad eighties movie moment—hoping that the last porcelain dog ornament was still there.

Although it is not Thanksgiving yet, Macy's is ramping up for the holiday season with an ad campaign called "Believe". So I dashed past banner after banner on which the word "Believe"—emblazoned in the red letters of an old-fashioned cursive script—popped out from a plain white background. The iconography was obvious enough; the red and white said candy cane, said Christmas, and there was even a star for the faithful to follow. Of course, the word "believe" referred not to any supernatural system of faith but to the story "Yes, Virginia, there is a Santa Claus", part of the Macy's mythology.

This sort of replacement of types of belief has always annoyed me, yet, as I fished through my wallet to find singles and purchased Macy's last porcelain dog ornament, I was participating in it. What was I doing except asserting that even purely material wishes come true, that loss and pain do not exist, that if we try hard enough we can live in a temporal, department-store utopia? I was working to give the impression that wish fulfillment is true. And that department stores and credit cards are the magical forces that grant wishes. I was giving my daughter a false sense of what is true and reliable and lasting, a false sense of the eternal, diametrically opposed to Saint John's vision of the Lamb still bearing the marks of slaughter but now standing upon the heavenly throne, surrounded by the twenty-four elders and the four living creatures (Rev 4:1–11, today's first reading; cf. Rev 5:6).

I suppose that the best approach would have been to tell my daughter the truth: the dog broke, and we replaced him, because we love her. Had I done this, I would have been giving her a Christocentric model of the universe. I would have been showing her that all material things are contingent; they reflect implicitly the image of the one who is not contingent, he who suffered and now stands on the throne.

But I am a coward. It is difficult to make any decision that probably results in a bawling child. For now I will leave her in illusion. Unless I am entirely mistaken about the nature of the universe, life will fix this illusion shortly. Loss and death cannot be long avoided. The message must be delivered, but sometimes I shrink from being the messenger.

Our Lord Jesus Christ, King of the Universe (Christ the King) (Rev 1:5–8; Ps 93:1, 1–2, 5; Jn 18:33b–37)

With the Feast of Christ the King, we come to the last Sunday in the liturgical year. This is the feast that, as the priest reminded us in the vigil Mass last night, Pius XI proclaimed to a war-ravaged Europe that was turning to fascism and communism to solve its problems, making idols of race, class, and nation. Pius XI issued this feast as a solemn reminder to the world that Christ, not any impersonal force or any power of our own making, is King of the Universe. That charity is stronger than power. That the true empire is that of righteousness and truth, and that any attempt to overthrow this Kingdom will be illusory. Christ forever reigns.

In today's readings, Jesus teaches, "For this I was born, and for this I came into the world, to testify to the truth. Everyone who belongs to the truth hears my voice" (Jn 18:37; this verse is the conclusion of today's Gospel reading, Jn 18:33b–37). Christ's words are fitting for the last Sunday of the liturgical year. The liturgy trains us to hear the voice of Christ, sensitizes us to perceive the truth. This verse and this feast sum up the purpose of the liturgical year.

If we've processed what the liturgy has been teaching us for the last year, then we've begun to realize that Christ is King of the Universe. We are coming to be the people who live with a primary allegiance to Christ and only a secondary allegiance to any political, social, economic, or academic power. If Christ is a King, then we are his Kingdom. As the second reading (Rev 1:5–8) reminds us, he has "made us into a kingdom, priests for his God and Father"; "to him be glory and power forever and ever" (6). We are beginning to realize (in the words of today's Responsorial Psalm) that God's universe "is firm, not to be moved"; his "decrees are worthy of trust indeed" (Ps 93:2, 5). In pondering God's ways through the year, we are not simply seeking emotive inspiration that will help us survive a frigid and cold universe; we are coming to perceive the world as it really is. This has been the goal of my yearlong experiment in liturgical living. But it takes every last Sunday of the year to get there.

Over the course of this last year, as I've tried to learn to think liturgically, I have grappled especially with two things: money and family. In this, I am simply the typical youngish (now middle-aged) American professional. My wife and I have established jobs and academic careers in which we are advancing. We have one child. We have been through Ph.D. programs at major secular universities. We know this story and we know where the narrative goes from here. You move into the elaborate but quirky house that serves as the physical symbol of both your material success and your commitment to aesthetics. You stop at one child because one child can be managed without a considerable hit to the finances; you can still manage the

European vacations and research trips that professors are expected to have, and you can afford to send the kid off to boarding school if he proves an inconvenience. You will still be able to make your work the center of your life, rather than family. Also, your colleagues will understand that—though you eccentrically wished to experience parenthood—you weren't being self-indulgent. You will still be contributing to world population reduction; you fit the terms of China's one-child policy.

The priest asked us to think yesterday about the kings we serve rather than Christ, and certainly the kings we serve are money (here we are like all Americans) and prestige (here we are very professorial). I can satirize this way of thinking, but this doesn't mean that I haven't internalized it, that it isn't always with me, that it doesn't whisper in my head like a false conscience. I know Emily struggles with the same thing.

To meditate upon the liturgy is to learn to reject this false conscience, to internalize instead the voice of Christ as truth. You show you've internalized the voice of Christ if you make decisions that show your allegiance to his Kingdom. As I've mentioned, the big issues for us—as probably for all young professionals entering midlife—have been money and family. And, as I've charted throughout this book, the liturgy has told us a counternarrative, a very different story, where the poor are blessed and love is generative, where we are to populate the earth, not to thin the human herd. And the liturgy has done so with oddly perfect timing. For instance, on the day when we thought we had found the perfect big house, the liturgy told us about the rich young ruler and the camel and the needle's eye.

And now it all comes to a head in this final week or two of the liturgical year. Listening to the logic of the liturgy, we reached the decision to stay in our smaller house in

an affordable neighborhood so we could manage to give
20 percent of our income to God and to the poor. Last
Wednesday, ten days from the end of the liturgical year,
we finished remodeling our kitchen to make this house
(our first house, purchased right out of graduate school)
the place we plan to stay for the foreseeable future. I
know this decision does not make us Saint Francis of Assisi
or Dorothy Day any more than our new openness to a
multichild family makes us the Duggar family from cable
TV's *19 Kids and Counting*, but it *is* a decision we would
not have made before. We are becoming different people
than we were a year ago.

We went to Saturday Mass this week and encountered
the Christ the King reading yesterday. So it happened that
on the day we assisted at the Mass for the Feast of Christ
the King, we received God's answer about family as well:
Emily is pregnant.

I hadn't even known that she was going to take a pregnancy test. She had noticed a few days ago that she was
late, but she was ready with a plausible explanation—"I
knew it. Early menopause. I meet all the symptoms"—so
we hadn't thought too much about it. Only this morning
lying in bed did she even start to wonder if she might possibly be wrong, but she still ruled out using a pregnancy
test ("It would just be a waste of money. I'm sure I'm in
early menopause. Cracked cistern"). So as I began upstairs
to dress and get ready for the day and Emily descended to
prepare breakfast, I had no idea anything significant was
about to occur.

But Emily had begun to wonder, and as I have said, for
her the moment for action is always now. She can't wonder about anything without doing it. "Chene, come *down*
here!" she shouted from the bathroom. I thought from her
troubled tone that something in the kitchen had broken

and was spewing water and that we were back to January. I ran quickly down the stairs, skipping steps, stumbled, and caught myself on the railing. She shoved a stick in my face: "Look at this!" The stick was right between my eyes, so I couldn't quite bring it into focus. I couldn't initially even process what I was being told. We were entering a different world, and I saw people as trees walking and couldn't grasp the country into which I was entering. But things begin to come into focus, and I begin to learn my way.

EPILOGUE: THE STORY WHICH
IS NOT A STORY

Just this once, I will break time. As we neared the end of the liturgical year, I realized that the liturgy was asking me to change how I told the story of my life, to rethink what I considered a good story. If you've made this journey with me, you too are questioning how you should look at your life and how you should make sense of the existence you are living. So I will close with this rumination on the liturgy's story and our story.

The second reading for the Twenty-Ninth Sunday in Ordinary Time (Heb 4:14–16) makes a famous statement about Jesus, one that baffles the modern reader: he was "tested in every way, yet without sin" (15). What, we ask, could it possibly mean to be tempted in all things but to resist? How can we narrate this? As a culture, we typically define depth and complexity of character in terms of giving in to temptation. A person who has been a drug or sex addict and then recovers balance in life is an interesting, edgy person; the person who has been sober and chaste since childhood is either too tedious to be noticed, or is an unreflective bigot, or is emotionally stunted, or is hiding something. The celebrity who has been through rehab has a compelling story plastered all over the television and the tabloids; the life of Saint Thérèse of the Child Jesus, "the Little Flower", would now be too dull to recall. She is a holy child, then becomes a nun, stays a nun, and dies. Where's the story? The journalist seeks in vain for an angle.

Back at Ohio State, I had a Christian former student who was getting a C or a D in a creative-writing class with another graduate teaching associate because he kept writing about Christian characters and his teacher basically hated Christians. He met with me because he wanted to know how to get a good grade in the class without selling out his convictions. I replied, "Easy. Make your Christian character a recovering alcoholic or drug addict who uses faith as a means of controlling his inner demons. Everyone likes inner demons, even if he doesn't like God. Even faith in God can be forgiven if you've got a few." The student went on to get an A in the course.

We find something suspect in *not* giving in to temptation. Oscar Wilde quipped long ago in *The Picture of Dorian Gray* that the only way to make temptations depart is to give in to them; we have internalized this as a cultural lesson. We have a basic sense that not to give in to temptation is not to be human, that one who was tempted like us, "yet without sin", hasn't really been tempted like us and has missed out on experiencing human complexity. A sinless Christ, we feel, can be only a mythological creature, without even being, like most myths, a good story. In this light, some of the more scandalous modern depictions of Jesus—*The Last Temptation of Christ*, for example—might represent an understandable impulse, wrongly channeled. They may create a sinful Christ in a misguided attempt to make Christ human and relevant to our needs and concerns, to create a Christ who fits our story.

But, as many scholars have noted, the Gospels redefine what a story is. They use the Roman literary forms reserved for narrating the lives of emperors and use them to tell the story of a Galilean peasant—a nonperson, as far as Rome is concerned. They redefine what heroism is (the Cross) and what constitutes victory (the Resurrection). Oscar Wilde wrote a poem about this as well, a serious poem about the Annunciation ("Ave Maria Gratia Plena"). In Wilde's poem, the speaker, well versed in pagan mythology, imagines that he will find the human conception of the deity to be an exciting, violent scene, probably a rape—and then is shocked at the quiet beauty of the scene unfolding before him.

Although I am far from sinless, I have wondered throughout these ruminations whether I really have a story. My sins are too dull, my transformations too quiet, my concerns—whether we should have another child, how one deals with middle age, and so on—too commonplace. But Hebrews tells us, the Gospels tell us, that the story which is not a story is *the* story. And in the liturgical year, as we experience this story day by day and project it out onto our lives, it becomes our story. This, perhaps, is what I've really been learning over the course of this liturgical year: my life—and yours—gains shape and direction, becomes a story and a story worth telling, only when read in light of Christ's story.